MATTHEW AARON NUGENT

Four Fingers and a Thumb

WESTBOW
PRESS
A DIVISION OF THOMAS NELSON

WestBow Press books may be ordered through booksellers or by contacting:

WestBow Press
A Division of Thomas Nelson
1663 Liberty Drive
Bloomington, IN 47403
www.westbowpress.com
1-(866) 928-1240

Because of the dynamic nature of the Internet, any Web addresses or links contained in this book may have changed since publication and may no longer be valid. The views expressed in this work are solely those of the author and do not necessarily reflect the views of the publisher, and the publisher hereby disclaims any responsibility for them.

Any people depicted in stock imagery provided by Thinkstock are models, and such images are being used for illustrative purposes only.

Certain stock imagery © Thinkstock.

ISBN: 978-1-4497-0644-9 (sc)
ISBN: 978-1-4497-0794-1 (e)

Library of Congress Control Number: 2010939310

Printed in the United States of America

WestBow Press rev. date: 11/08/2010

"For by one spirit we were all baptized into one body, whether Jews or Greeks, whether slaves or free, and we were all made to drink from one spirit. For the body is not one member but many."

(1 Cor. 12:13, 14)

I was having a bit of trouble thinking of where to start this and then one morning I came across this wonderful scripture and knew this would be the place. From childhood to within a few years ago I saw myself as an individual. One human being among millions, each with their own agenda or family or career and all going and flowing in independent directions. So many people living an existence that felt to me so disconnected and irrelevant that I was not sure what to do or where to go next.

I began studying medicine several years ago beginning with my tour in the U.S. Navy. As a burned out twenty something going part time to the local Community College and mowing lawns I wanted to get out of the small but addictive town in which I was raised. I joined the military in 1993 and was sent off to Orlando Florida to begin this journey. After becoming the Recruit Chief Petty Officer of my Division in boot camp I uniquely was given the opportunity to choose any school available and I chose the Medical Corps. The fast pace classes and upbeat pleasantries of Navy life in San Diego became a second love of mine. The weather, the comradary, the classes and the great fellow sailors I met all became a place I would love to go back to one day. Through these classes I started to see some truly amazing things. The human body and all of its wonder began to nest itself deep within my heart and soul as my new interest and career.

The Navy allowed me the opportunity to get the first level of understanding into the human body, the physiological mechanisms and the structures that base all body function, the systems that are at work within each and every one of us 24hrs a day without any need or assistance but the willingness to breath. Although each human is so unique and different from the other, so clearly separate and characteristically genuine one undeniable fact remains, we are all physiologically the same. For hundreds of years medical professionals have been dissecting and studying the human body from the tip of the longest hair to the smallest molecule and the atoms that complete us. Step by step detail by detail the science of tissue, organs, bone and fluids has developed with technology and has become one of the most well defined machines on earth. The fact that our hearts are continuing to beat independently from our brains, hour after hour, thirty six million beats each year pushing five quarts of blood through more than fifty thousand miles of veins, arteries and tubes, that we are currently digesting our last meal without any assistance, that we are making neurological transmissions faster than we can even realize, that the simple movement of a finger is generated in our brains, three pounds of tissue with thirteen billion nerve cells sending synapse at 90ft per second traveling through insulated fibers to the waiting finger at the end of an arm and that all of this is encased within a shell of regenerating skin that stretches and flexes with each movement and step. These things and millions more are happening every second of every day all around and within us and we never stop to notice. Each amazing human being not only operates on an unseen, undetectable battery pack, we also function on a complete subconscious level, making plans and decisions without even realizing it.

The human body although unique in DNA to each individual is structurally identical. The same tissue structures, organs, brain matter, cellular size and weight and scientific bases are the same. Without a personality, two human bodies lying side by side have no direct differences. Nothing can separate the two if not by name or some kind of identification. The DNA within each human being is of course unique in it's code but to individualize a person is to interact outwardly with characteristics we are identifying each and every day. We make a perception of those characteristics from those close to us at home, our family, the first impressions of a chance meeting on the street, the routine passing glances of those at work, the analyzing of those in which we challenge and that challenge us and surly the specifics in which we evaluate those of our leaders. Each second of everyday an outside stimulus enters our brains through one or more of the several interactive receptors we have placed around our body and consciously or unconsciously evaluates, identifies stores and makes decisions based on it. This is creating an opinion of the smell, site, sound, feel and vibration of that stimulus.

The living things that are around us represent themselves without choice. The trees although may be of different species are unique in themselves but cannot choose the color of their leaves. The flowers again are of many shapes and sizes but cannot pick the shape of their petals. Although all of the living things around us are special and unique in themselves they cannot interact and communicate directly with their surroundings. But we as humans are doing this constantly. Evaluating what it is that makes us feel a certain way. Even those that feel isolated, angry and at lose with society do so by processing their environment and influence and therefore choose to act out in a way that displays their vision of their individual self. Confidence is a show of self worth. The dress of a person believing that what they are representing is a character of earned status has a self image of success. The look of strength, sincerity, sadness, joy, anxiousness and fear are reactions to stimulus and processed thought through our brains based on our understanding of that position.

These pieces of character that are displayed amongst us all reflect our personality, inner being, self image and who we really are. As babies are born into a world of such massive newness with which nothing is labeled they must build without words an immediate understanding of their environment. The comfort of closeness can ease their confusion in the immediate birth but from that point forward the learning process begins by the reception of outside stimulus and the building of facts. The special sounds that become so attractive and known as a mothers voice or the smell of her perfume or the touch of a fathers hands all start to build within the mind of a child a vision of what is comforting. No words are chained together for communication but yet the simplest of things become clear. The learning process has already begun by knowing that feeling cold is uncomfortable and a blanket is the answer to the problem. The learning process carries on for years after. Sounds become words, words become sentences, recognition of pain and pleasure become a guide line for does and don'ts and slowly but surly the learning develops character and character develops self.

There are books upon books, millions of pages that hundreds of people have written describing the developing behavior and character of human beings. The Psychology of human behavior and the parts of the brain responsible for that personality, decision making and thinking calculations paints a picture of who we are and what we think we are all through the development of self. The personality of an individual for most people is seen as an intangible object but Psychology has created a more hands on guide to the structure of that personality. From the originator Sigmund Freud to today's creative writers and professionals delving deeply into the realms of Psychology to thoroughly give us a road map to its understanding we are capable of seeing once and for all the true Psychological aspect of personality and self. Not only are there breakthroughs in the practice of therapy and non-medication treatment but technology is opening a door that will allow for the intangible to be a solid object for all to see. The brain and its structures lie deep within the human skull and for hundreds of years the guess work became documentation and testing became limited. In today's world of technology we have the ability to look into the brain seeing things that have never been seen before taking inquiry and making it fact. The active and functioning brain of patients can be colorfully displayed on a monitor in three dimensional manner and moved, flipped, flopped and sliced without ever taking a scalpel to a hair on their head. Questions of brain activity, thinking processes, behavior, personality and many more psychological aspects of human activity can now be approached on a more confident less abrasive field. It was not that long ago when Insulin coma and shock therapy were answers to treatment of possible schizophrenic patients and today that is a thing of the past thanks to modern science.

The world of Physiology and the breakthroughs in Neurology have shown a new light on the three pounds of tissue within our skulls and between our ears. More and more clear and concise understanding of the full capabilities of the human brain are becoming bright and embracing with each dawning of the medical day. The trap of guess work slowly becomes a piece of history and the visions of non-threatening treatment zoom within our grasp with each horizon. Today not only are we able to think together putting the professions of Psychology and Neurology into one and adopting the new methods of study we are also able to see and accept new and amazing findings along the way. If there is a stage though in which technology over rides the practice of a profession than the profession becomes null but the skills of those designated to lead that field to another century can join those in technology and become capable of findings beyond our imaginations. We must embrace those days.

The years of Psychological study and development have created many amazing and fruitful concepts although we may be to the point in which the joint fields of Psychology, Neurology and Spirituality join hands, opening the door to findings in a combined field of study leading to truly amazing and un-approached concepts.

Human Physiology and technology has lead us into Brain Science in a manner that has never before been exposed. Neurology has brought to us a window into the amazing structure of the brain and all of its uniqueness. We have made leaps and bounds in brain science that have allowed us to further understand the three pounds of tissue within our skulls much more. Through Magnetic Resonance Imaging (MRI), Computerized Tomography(CT), Electroencephalograms (EEG), Electrocardiograms (EKG) and many other tests and machines we are able to finally see a three dimensional picture of the human body, heart and active brain. Slice by slice the pits and valleys of the brain become a picture and frame by frame a world so long undiscovered comes to life. The deeper the study goes into the brain, the more miraculous the findings are. In the past few years the Functional MRI has shown the brain activity within humans to be so specific that even the slightest thought of a butterfly is lit up like the fourth of July on a small monitor. The thought processes can be tracked through high lit areas of the brain from the introduction of the stimulus to the identifying features of the thought and the calculations of the out come. We can now better study the neuron, the nerve cell that is key to millions of activities within us and is replicated more than thirteen billion times throughout the brain, more than three times the number of people on the earth. These nerves function based on several things. Some chemicals within us are responsible for nerve function. Sodium and Potassium act as igniters for the action potential of a nerve cell sending a chain reaction down the limbs of the cell to properly send its signal. Others use other chemicals and some none at all. The heart sends an electronic charge from the top of the heart to the bottom constricting the muscle tissue hundreds of times a day without any assistance from the brain what so ever. The heart beats so independently that even some medications have been useless on the control of the rate and nothing short of cutting the nerves and replacing them with a pace maker has been the answer to an awkward and dangerous heart beat.

The guest of honor here is _**Energy.**_ The amount of energy within the human body is amazing. The fact that brain waves can be measured and detected, the heart can beat with no battery pack whatsoever, the neurons fire constantly through conscious and unconscious thought all day long is amazing in itself but with today's technology this energy can be identified, seen and measured. The mystery here becomes that if the amount of potential energy capable in the body can peak at a maximum amount but yet the amount of energy detectable through technology identifies an amount all together higher where does the extra energy come from? The human body can only produce so much energy and the remainder is the key. But *what* is that remaining energy and how do we isolate it and use it specifically?

Let's go on a *"What If"* kind of walk. If we can accept the Psychological aspects of human behavior and personality, the Physiological aspects of the human body and the scientific findings of Neurology as well as the details that each represent then we can accept the fourth category, the one of Spirituality. Can it be now, today when we determine that the energy within the human body is from a source other than science alone can answer? In Critical Care I have witnessed patients pass away but while they are alive the monitors display the electronic signals picked up by leads throughout the body and when the body looses life, the energy waves that are detectable by monitors and computers halt. The energy itself is no longer detectable within the flesh of the patient remaining. Where does the energy go? That measurable, tangible, hands on energy is gone. As people have had near death experiences they have seen themselves above their human body and at that point the monitors detecting the energy within the body rapidly decreases. The heart which beats independently from the brain looses it's stimulus as well and the body dies, but when the near death patient returns to the body below, the monitors once again pick up the energy signals and life returns. Could the spirit of the human body be the energy that is so clearly detectable within us? If we can determine that this energy can be depicted as the human spirit or soul than we can accept its origin and the creator of all life on earth.

If we have the ability to process a stimulus and then in the end use something we identify as "Free Will" to choose what to do with it next than what is that *conscience*, that *will*, that provides a nudge in either direction? Let's say that there is an energy that flows in and around all of us. It is an energy that is absorbed by all living things to allow growth, death and re-grow. It is an energy that can be detected through analysis and documented as a tangible object. It is an energy that through proper methods can be accessed and used within the human body and mind. ___The power of the Holy Spirit___. That spirit that was set free on this planet for all to use so many years ago is the same energy that encircles us each and every day. .

The answer is not JUST Psychology. Not JUST Human Physiology, not JUST Spiritual concepts. But ALL rolled into one to determine the most amazing thing of all. We have the ability to maintain and utilize a gift that has been here this whole time. The God given energy that surrounds each and every living thing, which also up until most recently, has been unseen and deniable. Let's think for a moment that we were able to *prove* the existence of God. Through the facts depicted in medicine and technology and then linking it all back to the only documentation that describes the existence of this energy, the

Holy Bible. An energy detectable within the human body that is above and beyond any chemical or natural one ever produced within us. The barriers of personality than can be broadened by the possibility of past lives in which our spirit, our energy has been here before. Our internal being that assists the human body to function on earth allowing us to speak, move and exist but not only from the personality of the developed mind but of one that has compiled past life experience into who we are today. A combination of flesh and spirit energy.

This is the adventure in which I have chosen to undertake. *The proving of spirit! The proving of God!*

Section One

The Fizz in Human Phys

*T*he depths and specifics of Human Physiology are many and the details may even bore some but in this section I wanted to supply enough information of the human body to clearly see the physical aspects of its functions in particular the brain itself. The mechanisms of the body are all so special in each job they have to do that not one of them is really more important than the other. One of the unique things is how they all work within each other and complete a part of the entire job of keeping the human body a functional and healthy machine. Although so many things are responsible for the development and maintenance of the body, the body alone cannot operate without energy. This section talks about the body structure a bit to help us understand the miracle of how this skin wrapped being works as an individual human machine. The deeper, more scientific aspects of the human body may not be what is needed here, but a physiological understanding of us is. So here we go on a walk through the body.

The bones structure of the human body most certainly acts as a base for the whole support aspects. There are about 200 bones all inner linking to each other through masses of tendons and cartilage. All growing from a young age of calcium and marrow to not only allow for a strong structure but also to aide in the replenishing of blood cells. A frame that without it would leave a jiggly pile of tissue behind. From the feet to the top of the skull, these bones have grown in equal patterns to allow not only for shape but proportioned height and width. The bones reflect stature and movement, size and strength and although hidden behind the layers of skin they also are a detrimental piece of our existence. Our feet alone have more than 40 *tarsals, metatarsals* and *filanges*. These bones all serve a purpose for flexibility, stability and movement. Because we have many pounds of body weight dispersed in a rather awkward stance, we need our many bones in our feet to flex and shift the weight allowing us to stand and not fall over. Try standing on your feet and NOT allowing for them to flex with the shift of weight. Without taking a step to prevent it we would fall to the floor. The bones in the feet have been uniquely engineered for the purpose of us standing upward. The feet themselves are a direct reflection of the pre-thought that went into the way we move, walk and run. The feet alone show that without something as simple but magnificent as their structure we already would not be what we are today.

When we think of our feet, we think of them as two meaty, less attractive features of our body but if it wasn't for them we would have no way of transporting ourselves physically or even doing something as simple as standing. Not only do the bones allow for so much advantage but the pads of our feet also help us. The tough skin that grows so thick and resilient allows us to walk for hundreds of years barefoot and not tear them up so much. Imagine running through the woods in bare feet but with tender soft pads below surly would be painful. This is another easily forgettable aspect of the feet. Makes you want to take a bit more care of them doesn't it?

Stemming up from the feet are several long bones providing strength to further our stability. In our legs we have some of the strongest bones in the body and certainly some of the largest. The leg bones give us our support for the upper torso. The largest of the leg bones is the *femur* (thigh) bone. This bone is the one that links our hips to the rest of the lower half. The femur in all humans and animals as well is one of the heaviest and most durable bones in the body. For good reason too, the femoral artery runs along that bone on the deep inside of our inner thigh and supplies blood to the entire lower extremities. This artery is so important that in the case of a tear or cut of that blood vessel, we could die from blood loss in less than five minutes. This bone must be as strong and as robust as it is for the sake of protecting a blood source that is key to our existence. So not only do we have a large bone in the upper part of the leg, we also have a tuff enforcer and protector of the femoral artery. The more we envision these key aspects of the human body the more we see the specially engineered details that make nothing more than a miracle in itself.

Further up the body are many other bones and crevices that are special but next we come to the beginning structure of the spine. Our spine is a combination of twenty five inner linked bones called *vertebrae* and rubber like discs that cushion and separate them. This structure really starts to take shape within three to four weeks of fetal development. The spinal column is already clear on ultrasound machines at that point. These twenty five bones begin at the bottom of the back and flow up through the center and into the base of the skull. At the bottom of our back we have seven lower or *lumbar* spine bones that begin the trek upward. These bones allow for support of the lower back and thanks to their size and shape they also support the remaining spine and structure above. Your lower back has surly ached and has been irritated at some point in your life but considering its job it is no surprise. These bones have thick calcium based features and with the rubber like discs between them movement of the lower half of our backs becomes fluid. Up from the lumbar spine is the collaboration of twelve *thoracic* vertebrae providing support and movement to the middle back. These bones, like the ones below them are also there for support of the upper body but become smaller as they approach the neck. The unique thing about these bones is that they have a special assistance to the ribs themselves. The protectors of the chest, the ribs, wrap around and meet in the middle at a plate called the *sternum* and with the thoracic spine become a hefty cage of support for the heart and lungs. The Twelve thoracic spine bones attach to the twelve ribs and further provide for movement and support of the heavy chest. The final piece of the spine climbs from the top of the thoracic to the base of the skull. These are the seven *cervical* spine bones which are special in the movement and support of the head itself. All of the movement of the skull relies on the strategically placed bones of the neck. These bones are giving us the flexibility of movement but most of all the protection of the top of the spinal cord itself. The entire back, all twenty five spinal bones, including the *coccyx* at the very bottom are doing an amazing job of support but something perhaps even more delicate is sheltered within them. The spinal cord is the delicate and intricate link between our brains and the rest of the body. These spinal bones are not just performing one job but many all at the same time. Support, movement, protection and stability all within three categories of creatively placed and engineered bones.

The ribs wrapping along the sides of the chest and coming to the middle are a cage of iron will to protect that beautiful muscle we know of as the heart. The ribs are firmly linked to the sternum allowing for flexion when we breathe and bounce around but also are tough in the barrier of the chest cavity itself. The lungs and heart would have no defense accept for the rib bones evenly separated from each other with just enough space that movement is clean and support is functional. These bones are serving perhaps one of the most important assignments of the bone structure itself. I can't think of a better way to protect our heart and lungs than by building a cage around them. But the cage concept was already inside of us in the form of the ribs themselves. As the shoulders carry out from the center of our chest and spine we come to our lanky and useful arms.

At the shoulders our arms are set into a socket that gives a range of motion in broad circles and wide arcs. The shoulders give way to the upper arm, the *humorous* bone which lead down to the *radius* and *ulna*, the forearm bones. The humorous bone is a protector like the femur in the thigh. Along the inside of this bone is an artery called the *brachial*. This artery provides blood for the entire upper extremity, all the way to the fingertips and once again if it is cut or severed can lead to a deadly amount of blood loss. Between the upper and lower arms, the elbow joins them allowing for flexion and extension. At the end of the line are of course the bones of the hands. These, like the ones of the feet are small and many, performing great and amazing tasks. The bones in the hands are called the *carpals*, *metacarpals* and *filanges* and are allot like the feet. Although the feet are similar in many animals, the hands of the human are special in the way of opposable thumbs. The ability to grasp things and lift, cradle and move objects is unique to us alone. Though some creatures have similar features, only humans have the digits like we do. The hands seem to be one of the sets of tools we have that portray as much meaning as they do use. For all time our hands have built up and torn down, pulled in close and pushed away, waved in gestures of good will and bid farewell to those going off into the day. We have used our hands to create what our minds have given us in thought and ideas. We have been leaders of soldiers with the return of a stiff salute and a destroyer of people by pushing the buttons of destruction. The hands we have are the gifts of communication and the writers of books, the holders of hands and the planters of trees. The fifty some bones placed strategically throughout the palms, wrist and fingers allow for movement assisted by the strength of muscles along our arms. Again like the feet, so many movements and tasks become impossible without each significant part. Each finger assists the others with just enough percent of care that as a whole the weakest of digits becomes a fist of brute strength. Through hundreds of years human lives have been altered through the use of our hands and once again with four fingers and a thumb, history again will be written.

As our shoulders lead us to the bones of the neck once more, we follow the cervical spine to the base of the skull, perhaps the most important protective structure of all bones of the body. The skull houses the brain within ten specific bones each joining the other in a manner which allows for strength and movement. The skull also houses the eyes in cave like protective orbits and the jaw bone for eating, speaking and facial structure. The bones of the skull have begun growth within the mother's womb and continued to grow concurrently until the early twenties. The sutures between the skull bones allow for growth and flexion as the brain becomes larger in size. The skull sits perfectly on the *atlas* bone at the very top of the cervical spine and allows for rotation and a balanced fit. The brain itself is so delicate and soft that nothing short of the strong bones of the skull can house this wonderful organ. The frontal bone of the skull at the forehead portion of the head is one of the strongest bones of the body and for good reason. We certainly have been the victim of a solid bump on the head or been whiteness to a child's swan dive off of a swing set. The back of the skull is the occipital bone protecting the back and lower section of the brain and brain stem. Acting like a helmet, the skull withstands amazing pressure, breaks and bruises but without it the consequences would be ultimate death.

The front of the skull opens to the eye sockets, nasal cavity and mouth. We surly are aware of the use of each of these organs but the magic is what is not seen from the front. Our eyes amazingly grow in unison with each other and at the same pace of the skull and brain. Both eyes have a *cornea, pupil* and *iris* that act as the lenses in which vision begins. The eyes as so many people have said are the windows into the soul. The eyes have been tools for navigation, stimulus reception and even communication for hundreds of years. As the eyes are used in vision, rays of light bring an image into the retina inverting it exciting nerve impulses in *rods* and *cones*. The image then follows pathways down the optic nerve to the midbrain area and visual radiations make intricate connections in the *occipital* (back of the brain) lobe. The signal actually carries from the front of the head through the eyes to the back of the brain to be processed. Our eyes send the signals down nerve fibers that cross at the midbrain and end at opposite sides of the rear of our head. The right ends up on the left and the left on the right. Our eyes have been an undeniable miracle in which science and technology still cannot replicate. Not only is the eye so special in its structure but a wonderful piece of our face. The eyes for years have been a device for vision but a tool for attraction and a guide of faith. So many people have been said to read a persons thoughts through the eyes, to be able to feel recognition of pain or sadness, of joy or ease. Although the muscles around our eyes allow for movement and constriction around the eye itself, the eyes have been a remarkable pathway to inner being. Of all senses, vision has been the one that people seem worst off without. The depths of distance, the identity of danger, the approach of a loved one and the colors of the world around us all bring an understanding of life to new meaning. When we see a recreation of a person in a museum or in the movies it seems we go directly to the eyes to determine the life likeness of the creation. Our eyes tell all and for that a miracle was performed within itself.

Dropping down below the eyes is that feature that so many of us take for granted; at least I did until I understood the internal function. The nose itself is primarily a filter for inhaled air and a port for the release of mucus. The magic of smell actually happens in the *olfactory* system just inside the nasal cavity. The space behind the nose holds bones called *turbinates*. Above the turbinates is a bone called the *ethmoid* that acts as a floor to the brain and a roof to the nasal cavity. When we breathe in, the individual smells are picked up by nerve fibers that reach the surface of the ethnoid bone or brain floor and relay these smells as signals to the brain to process them. Needless to say, the process of smell will then be affected by the inflammation or mucus covered walls of the sinus cavity, thus during colds our sense of smell is diminished. One of the amazing things about the sense of smell is that the individual aroma can be breathed in, processed through the nerve fibers in the nasal cavity, relayed to the brain and then identified but also triggers a memory related to that smell. I spent a day walking through the mall not too long ago and visited a candle store. All of the multi colored candles were displayed in baskets each with a different label describing the scent. As I picked up each one, I would close my eyes and see what memory if any was triggered by the smell. I found myself reliving some wonderful memories from holidays past to the smell of beach front afternoons back in San Diego. The sense of smell allows us to paint a picture of what the aroma is and teaches us how to isolate yet another amazing ability we have been given.

Along with smell, our mouths act along the same manner senses of taste and texture. Our mouth of course has an endless list of use. Again like the nose it is in the front of the face so clear to see but yet the miracles happen within it. Our lips help to shape sounds from our vocal chords to become words, pucker up to give a kiss, and squeeze to develop a whistle or keep food from falling carelessly from our mouth. The muscles around our mouth are many but the *orbicularis oris* and the *buccinators* make an amazing contribution to all of the mouths activity. We have about 32 teeth which when in good condition can tear and mash our food to a swallowable consistency. One of the amazing things though is the saliva glands lying under our tongues. These glands secret saliva to help break down food immediately in our mouth while we are chewing. Have you ever been chewing a piece of bread and think how sweet it tastes? That's mostly due to the sugars released while breaking down the starch in the bread. When we think of something that would be tasty or are preparing for dinner, we already have an increase in saliva just thinking of food. Our brain detects that it is almost time to eat so the glands release and our mouth waters. Once the food enters our mouth another amazing thing happens, the taste buds relay signals to the brain identifying the sweet, sour, bitter, and salty taste. All along the top of the tongue we have little receptors that sense the chemicals in the food and that's how we know the flavor. There are four different locations on our tongue that have these receptors. Needless to say a bad burn on the tongue from hot coffee can make the taste receptors loose their strength. The mouth has its intake responsibilities but surly the output seems to be what we remember the most. Our voice has an impact on human life that at times seems more powerful than the weapons we build. Over many life times people have used the words from our minds to create and destroy as much or more than our hands ever have. The voice we use can also comfort, reward and create ideas. By going backwards through our mouths we go to the vocal chords which stretch and flex from the muscles around them modifying the sound that comes from them. Our brain has a location called the Wernicks area that processes speech and sends signals to the muscles in order to flex or relax them making the sound we want. So many great people have been known for the speeches they have made and the inspirational paths they have sent others on. Our mouths have been responsible for what seems sometimes to be getting in front of our brains but in actuality nothing can be processed in speech without it coming from the brain first. Along this trip of the body we are building part by part an understanding of the brilliance and love such a creator must have. There is so much to talk about here but we will get more into it the further we go.

Parked so perfectly on the sides of our head are the sound receivers called the ears. Again the ears themselves act more as the satellite dish then the receivers themselves. The sound will come from around us and enter the ear drum causing it to vibrate, but the vibrations are incredibly small. Some are frequencies as small as one billionth of a centimeter, much less than the diameter of a single hydrogen atom. Little bones in the ear called ossicles vibrate sending the sound waves into the fluid inner ear. The sound travels into a liquid in the inner ear exciting nerve endings carrying nerve impulses to the brain. The brain processes those impulses at an alarming rate and forms facts from them to allow for understanding of that sound itself. Not only is all of that happening at an amazingly high rate of speed, even the slightest sounds, given a healthy inner ear, are detected and processed. What an amazing thing, this ear is. So many delicate, tiny pieces all working together to create something so unbelievable. Small bones, fluid membranes, nerve fibers all acting as amplifiers and processors representing one of the amazing miracles of sense. This is another undeniable gift.

All of these wonderful parts so far are wrapped in a covering of skin that is also the largest organ in the body. Clearly our skin grows and stretches with our bodies from the beginning of conception to the point we pass. Our skin is made of millions of cells that have the ability to regenerate and assist with the healing process. This tuff coat of skin holds all of our organs in place and even acts as a warming blanket as well as a cooling device. The skin has thousand of pores that use fluids to lubricate the skin to keep it healthy and sweat glands that release water to cool down the surface. About twenty square feet of tissue weighing around seven pounds covers us. All along the tissue there are little mechanisms that assist with keeping us alive and well. Some parts of the skin also produce antibodies to help keep out and fight foreign proteins. Along the skin also are millions of receptors. These receptors can pick up feeling through touch and send at an amazing pace signals to the brain to process them. These sensors are all over the skin from head to toe. The slightest touch or the slide of a breeze can stimulate these sensors and send a recognized signal up and away. Along the skin, just below the surface, millions of small blood vessels called capillaries fortify the many layers of tissue with all of the nutrients and oxygen that it needs. These capillaries also release white blood cells to help fight against foreign antibodies and infection. When we cut the skin and these blood vessels release fluid, they also have blood clotting cells that will block up the leaks and stop the bleeding. As we grow from children to adults our skin follows us, stretching and developing with every inch and fitting us through the rest of life. Although at times we grow faster inside than our skin does outside, it still continues to protect us for all time. This is one of the amazing pieces of the body that has so much complexity but to take the time breaking it all down would turn this book into a human physiology class, not really the objective so we will move on.

Deep within the body are several organs, all responsible for a job keeping the body a working machine. From the very first chew our bodies are digesting and extracting the nutrients from the food we eat. The tubes and tunnels that the food goes down are specially created to flex with the swallowing process. The ridges along the esophagus assist in the delivery of food to the stomach and once there the breakdown carries on. The chemicals in the stomach allow for the food to become liquid and then sent to the locations of the body to finish digestion. A remarkable part of this process is that it can all happen without our attention. Once the food enters the stomach, the remaining stages all take place independently. When we drink fluids they enter the stomach and are then passed through the lining of the stomach and released into the blood stream. This happens rather quickly as well. We can drink a twenty ounce soda and within twenty minutes or so release the remaining fluid through urine. The good nutrients are kept in the body and digested for the body use as fuel and the remaining is sent away in waste. Many of the organs in the body secrete enzymes and chemicals to assist with the digestion of food and liquids and with each and every one of them we build a healthy system. Once the nutrients enter the blood stream, it can be delivered to their destinations and released into the muscle, tissue or other organs for their final stop. The term "you are what you eat" comes from what the body does with the food that we eat. If we eat a lot of fatty foods, the body stores them in places that end up being extra padding. The food that we eat ends up in the muscles and tissues of the body so if it is healthy we stay strong and durable but we also can become weak and sick with the consumption of unhealthy food. The more exercise we do, the more our body burns the fluids in our muscle tissue and blood stream and so therefore we need to replace them with beneficial proteins in order to grow and stay strong. Although so many of the organs in our body have processes that are special and intricate we will touch on some of the most influential. This human factory has the capability of detecting what is necessary to keep and what to get rid of. Our kidneys have about 1,700 quarts of blood flow through them each day. Of all of that blood flow, carrying the fluids that we ingest, we excrete through the filters of the kidneys about one and a half quarts of urine a day. The kidneys have a lot of responsibility and clearly without them our bodies would become toxic and fail.

Our two lungs lie on either side of the chest cavity. These organs are several pounds of special oxygen transferring tissue. Around and within the lungs is a lining called the pleura. The pleura glide and slide along its surfaces allowing for the lungs to expand and contract without trouble. The tissue of the lungs is also very vascular in that they have a high number of small blood vessels flowing in and around the tissue. The air that we breathe in is warmed on its way to the lungs and goes into the lungs through branching tubes called bronchi. Once the air is in the lungs there are small sacs on the lung walls called alveoli that make gas exchanges. The oxygen is pulled from the air and exchanged with carbon dioxide which is sent out back through the throat and mouth. The oxygen is sent through the blood stream and released through the tiny capillaries in the tissues all around and within the body. Our skin, organs, brain and bone all rely on the circulation of oxygen in order to live. The exchange of these gasses in the lungs is what allows us to have a healthy and functional body. The reduction of oxygen entering the blood stream due to damage of the lungs or the overwhelming presence of harmful chemicals or gasses will majorly deplete the health of the body. The lungs are responsible for providing oxygen to the most vital organs of the body, mainly the brain. Once the oxygen rich blood circulates to the brain, the capillaries release the oxygen into the tissue and strengthen the cells within the tissue. These cells without proper oxygen will die and the surrounding skin becomes necrotic or dead. Needless to say the quality of air we breathe is a major influence to the health of the human body. With the understanding of the lungs comes now one of the most wonderful parts of the human body, the heart.

Our heart is a tough is remarkably tough hollow muscle about the size of your fist. The heart is an electrically stimulated muscle that fills, squeezes and circulates blood for the entire body. The heart beats about 70 times per minute and continues for the duration of our life time. The heart starts beating by the fourth weak after conception. In the adult the heart pumps about five ounces of blood per stroke, or four thousand gallons a day. The work done by the heart in twelve hours could lift a sixty five ton weight a foot into the air. The right side of the heart receives blood coming in from the body and sends it to the lungs to get rid of the carbon dioxide. The left side of the heart receives the blood from the heart or oxygenated blood and sends it to the rest of the body to be replenished. Our heart, like any other muscle gets stronger the more it works out. The more the heart beats as it develops, the stronger it gets. Over worked hearts though can grow like our arms do when we lift weights, but too much work can make the heart over sized and cause problems. The heart carries on allowing itself to rest between beats and even a little while pumping. Both sides of the heart beat in unison, first the auricles than the ventricles. The stages of heart beat in which one rests and the other pumps and visa versa are the upper and lower numbers of the blood pressure. This reading is what medical staff uses to evaluate the productivity of the heart. The heart beat itself is the electrical stimulation from the top of the hear muscle (the SA node) carrying on to the bottom of the heart (the AV node). This undetectable battery pack is sending the impulse independently from the brain as if running completely on its own. This electrical current is measurable and monitored by computers and leads placed on the chest. When any muscle is shocked with electricity it will contract just like the heart is when the current is released from the top to the bottom. One of the mysteries of this process is where this energy comes from. The heart is one of the organs begging to tell its tale. An undeniable example of an energy that is maintained within us that is above and beyond the physiological boundaries. Although we are unable to put a label on the hearts energy we are able to see it as an existing object measurable and real. This is a perfect instance in which the energy within the body is found but unanswered for. This is a source that is beyond science and now identified as the human spirit. Through all of the years of existence we have had undeniable evidence of spiritual energy blipping across the screens of heart monitors and all for granted. But today is a new day, a chance in which science and our faith can merge to a new understanding and approach not only the recognition of this energy but the study of it and its meaning. Not only is this a perfect opportunity for us to use the energy free flowing through us we also can utilize its source and become stronger. Imagine if you will the energy contained within us, currently being isolated for things like heart beat, being increased to the point in which our body's energy takes physical and mental ability to all new highs. The opportunities are endless and right before us inside our very own bodies.

This same energy is not just in the heart but all through the brain as well. The brain is using electrical stimulus through the neurological system constantly. The brain is sending and receiving information through the nerves and spinal column of our body even as we speak. As the though of movement begins in the brain it is released through fibers in the back of the brain down the spinal column and to the limb that is to move. This is happening at ninety feet per second, rushing through us on an electrical current that is wired a lot like the house that we live in. Imagine if the fuse box in the garage was the brain and all of the wire running from the brain is the spinal column and all of its branches. When the electricity is released from the fuse box down through the wire and to the light bulb in the kitchen, the electricity finishes the circuit and returns to the fuse box. In the same manner the brain sends a signal down through the spinal cord to its destination for use. The spinal cord, like the main wire coming into the fuse box is a thick bundle of fibers. If you were to cut this wire you could see hundreds of smaller wires all within the big one. The same is with the spinal cord, thousands of nerve strands all with an individual destination is within one bundle. The fibers for the movement of the hand branch off down the shoulder and into the lower extremity, then follows back up the arm and back to the brain for the reception of stimulation. The spinal cord has insulation all around it like the plastic on the outside of wire. This insulation prevents the escaping of energy, in a way shorting out the circuit. Along the nerve cell there is also a protective covering called the myelin sheath. This cover does the same, insulating the fiber from escaping impulse that is sent down the fiber from the source. By looking at the spinal cord it is clear that the repair of such an amazing device is very difficult if not impossible at this point. Surgeons have attempted the repair of the cord but each fiber is individual to specific locations in the body and the direct re-link of the fibers becomes the problem. So the end result is limited and non fluid motion. The nerve fibers that are cycling energy through us constantly are another example of this spirit. Again this energy is measurable and detected through out the body and mainly the brain.

The source of thought, the birth of ideas, generation of movement, files of memory, the balance of chemicals, vision, hearing, voice, dreams, recognition of love and hatred, pain and pleasure and every possible human activity is strategically balanced within the brain. In an fMRI (functional magnetic resonance imaging) machine at Cambridge University a patient named Mary is lying on the backboard of the big, white machine resembling a spaceship or time machine. She has had severe brain trauma from an accident several years prior and has been under the special care of nurses and doctors all along. Mary can't move or talk or control her facial movements. Along this path of medical care her family is concerned for her mental status and her future. Options for the removal of life support have entered the conversation many times. Like many other brain trauma patients Mary is thought to be in a vegetative state and has not the brain function of a human being any longer. Although as the large MRI machine begins its cycle a voice from the control room is heard easing Mary's fears and explaining the procedure. The voice asks Mary to imagine playing tennis, which was her favorite sport and was quite good at it. As the monitors display a three dimensional picture of her brain a glow of yellow and red begins to appear. The more she thinks of her tennis game, the brighter and larger the spots become. As the image in Mary's mind becomes more vivid the locations of the brain that are responsible for movement and coordination begin to flood with light. In Mary's mind now she is dashing after tennis balls on the courts of Wimbledon and sending powerful shots down the lines for a breathtaking win. Mary is fully alive and stronger in thought than ever. Mary may have lost her ability to function on many levels but in her mind she could hear, process thought, imagine and even process speech. Mary could hear the conversations around her all along about letting her go from life and today she scurries around in her wheelchair living a proud life. In similar situations stroke patients are in a state of complete mental shut down. The bleeding in the brain has forced the functions of the brain to be reduced to an extreme minimum. Within the brain there are protons that when further excited by the MRI machine they will show up as high lit areas of the brain. The protons themselves, energy in fine form are seen within the brain tissues actively cycling through generating thought and processing information. This is an energy source that releases through the body assisting with the slightest of movements all the way to the leaps and bounds of a track runner. The energy itself links portions of the brain through nerve pathways so that all lobes and sections of the brain can communicate. All through the brain there are specific locations designated for certain use. Locations for speech allows for the recognition of words and the linking of meaning and further to the generation of responses all in the matter of milliseconds. Our brains have grown and developed to process data at an alarming speed, giving us the ability to do many things at once. The nerves within the brain and all along the body whether sending or receiving signals are a highway of speeding light. Little darts of electrical generated stimulations going up and down the spinal cord like cars on a busy freeway. The brain engineers these and without tire, continues to work all day and all night even as we sleep.

The brain itself contains about twelve billion nerve cells each having the potential to reach many others. The possible individual links through this circuitry in the brain are in the whereabouts of one septillion. That is a one with twenty four zeros after it. The brains capacity is by far those most complex and mockavalient gift to man. The brains appearance is a bit less attractive than its performance though. With folds and crevices all along the surface, the brain bears an appearance of a walnut. Although the strange formations are not much to look at, they increase the surface area immensely and allow for landmark identification as well. The brain also has a deep vertical fissure or valley that divides the brain into two halves. Other fissures separate the brain into lobes. For instance the vision processes in the back of the brain in the occipital lobe, hearing and smell are located on the side of the brain in the temporal lobe and sensory and motor centers are on a section across the top of the brain covering both sides. Over the years of neurological study many parts of the brain have been identified but a lot is yet to be uncovered. Through the entire brain there are billions of nerves all linking and acting in a special manner and performing transmissions. Some of these nerves look like trees without leaves, several stems and branches reaching out to further cover an area of the brain. These nerves will send a signal from a specific part of the brain and then nerve by nerve the signal will continue until it reaches its final destination. Imagine seeing a red bird on a tree branch. The image enters the eyes, each taking in a separate layer of the object and converts the image into signals for the optic nerve to send on. The signal traces down the nerve fiber, through the center of the brain and is received at the back of the brain. From there the links carry to the portions of the brain that hold facts of the image. The color, shape, size and any other specifics of the image are extracted from memory which is compiled over years of learning. Once all of the specifics are gathered the information is processed and the name, if known, of the bird is retrieved. All of this is happening through the intricate circuitry of the nerves within the brain. We can process these things while carrying on a conversation, walking a path, talking on the phone or many other activities. So not only is the processing of the bird image happening at an amazing speed, all of the other neuro transmitters are firing as well. These computer like calculations are happening thousands of times a day. Never slowing enough to notice but continuing to function even when we are unaware. These electronic transmissions are firing away without being plugged into a wall. Without being assisted by a portable battery pack and with no need to recharge except for periods of sleep. In the deepest core of the brain there are formations called the Amygdala and the Hippocampus. The source of the names for these areas is beyond me but is certainly easy to remember. In college when I would try to remember where in the brain the memory was located I would imagine a big hippo sitting on a bench thinking very hard in a college courtyard like setting and sure enough *Hippocampus* would come flying into mind. Well deep within this area memories are filed away and accessed through thought no different than the facts of the red bird earlier. The tissue of this area is different than the surrounding tissue and holds a much different shape. The hippocampus receives signals from the nerves in the association cortex which in essence is one of the first locations used for the formation of thought. From the early stages of learning our hippocampus retains knowledge and builds a computer base of information for us to process future thought. When we process any stimulus from outside our selves, weather it is by touch, smell, taste or sound, the information is processed by what we have already learned in order to make a conclusion as to what that stimulus is. Without facts from the past stored in our brains the final outcome would be an unrecognized object and a new formation of facts would be built. Our memory has the massive data retention and does this in a mysterious manner. The memory and the structure of it are still under a lot of study but some amazing breakthroughs in science are taking place today. Lets take a *"what if"* walk again. What if science could engineer a biological microchip that uses cells in a gel substance to process millions of bits of information all with the stimulus of energy. On a glass slide in a lab lies a manmade computer made directly of cells. Now think of that same pact of cells retaining information that can be extracted at a later time. Information that is stored within cells for future extraction. Now imagine the same type of structure within your brain in the form of memory. That structure is most certainly already there. Our memories are planted deep within our brains and are built day by day experience by experience from childhood to adulthood and beyond. All of our learning finds a spot within linkable brain cells and is extracted when needed to form a memory. The science of biological microchips is real but we had it all along within our brain tissue.

Through this section of human physiology it is clear that the body and all of its mechanisms are a miracle in its creation. The cells in their structures and ability to regenerate, the blood flowing continuously through our vessels and veins, the organs working endlessly without direct influence from the outside world, the nerve fibers running like engineered tracks through the body and most certainly the intricacies of the brain and its ability are a gift of creation from way beyond a pond cells mutation. This is an amazing structure of thought and detail, of holistic proportions and spiritual engineering. Still yet so many questions unanswered and layers left to be pulled back but still undeniably beyond anything ever imagined possible. Even reading this material is a miracle in itself with all of the things happening at once tying the ability to coordinate neurological processes into a fine tunes electrical orchestra. We have found out how our bodies heal and how the immune systems fight bacteria and foreign cells. We have documented the energy found within and around our hearts and have come to the conclusion that certain levels of that and other energies are un accounted for. By taking every chemical that can be used to produce energy or neurological stimulation and burning it all at one time, which would be physiologically impossible, all of the energy created would be markedly below the amount of detectable potential energy in the body through measure. The reason that this information is not routinely published is because of the unaccountability of the energy. The question surely remains than, if the energy is not created in the body, where does the energy come from? Could we be pulling energy from around us? In the 1920's Dr. T. Henry Moray built a free energy device with no power input but was able to produce 50,000 watts of energy for several hours. In a highly documented demonstration, Moray's Radiant Energy Device lit thirty five light bulbs and a one thousand watt iron by tapping an invisible, universal sea of energy. The device used 29 transistor like, cold vacuum tube "valves" that trapped the incoming energy until it reached a high wattage. Could this be the energy source that we pull from for internal bodily power? It has been studied and found that a *loss* of energy may be more detectable than the initial introduction of it. An actual mass of energy loss was found during an experiment weighing patients as they passed away. The study was done in 1907 that measured specific weight of dying patients and at the time of death the body of the patient decreased in weight by about three quarters of an ounce. Each consistently loosing the same amount of weight once the monitors could no longer detect energy within the body. The energy within us has to have some kind of mass even if it is the slightest bit of an ounce. At the point when this study was done, the technology to measure the patients was outdated resulting in a possibility that there was more than an ounce of weight lost. On today's hospital beds, weight scales are electronic and calibrated very tightly. So a test done on today's terms may even show a more significant change in mass.

So now we have what it takes to continue our probe into the understanding of what that energy is. We now are ready for finding out not only what that energy may be but how it assists us with the identity of self and the spirit within that joins our bodies of flesh to become a unique and special individual.

To further understand our individuality we also need to see the Psychological side of personality and self development. That is where we go next, into the Psychological self......

Section Two

The Psych of Self

I know from my personal experience any time that I've spent in and around Psychology has been either in the classroom or related to one of my many life struggles. Being willing to be open to methods of self analyzation can be quite the task but well worth it in the end. I think a lot of us try to find out who we are later in life rather than who we *were* when we were young and most susceptible to influence. Through my life I've had challenges that could make or break me in more ways than one. Experiences that I would not ever wish on my worst enemies and most certainly are glad they are in my past. I was in an accident when I was fifteen. My best friend and I were riding our bikes down the side of a busy road when a truck whose driver miss judged passing another car, over corrected and ran into us. I was knocked down but my friend was ran over and unfortunately killed. The visions of that memory will always be in detail clearly until the day I die and certainly even after. I remember thinking to myself years later that my life seemed to skip like a record on a turn table, the outer rings being young life and spinning year by year into the center towards the end of life. That record seemed to skip several years for me and I found myself feeling as if I was thirty instead of fifteen. My teenage years were missing. I was feeling the stresses of an older man rather than enjoying the freedoms of teenage life. This was one instance in my life that I would reflect back on during my individuation process, my look into my inner being to further understand myself and my shadow. Years had passed and my undirected lifestyle led me to the U.S. Navy. I packed the little I needed and left my hometown to find something new and fulfilling. I met a young lady in Kenosha Wisconsin and we quickly became close and decided that we should get married. Our amazing daughters were born soon in the years to follow and two amazing girls they are. All along the cover of this book are the faces of the two people on this earth that make my heart sing and are two more things in my life that I have recognized as direct influences in my awakening. As the years went by my wife was pregnant with our third child. In the back of my mind I hoped so dearly for a son. The ideas of baseball games, playing football in the yard and all of the things my dad did with me sat waiting for the opportunity to be played out with my own son. My best friend that died in the biking accident when I was a boy was named Eric so I planned to pass the name Eric Matthew to my own son one day. That time came when Eric Matthew was born. He was healthy and strong at first but his lungs were giving him trouble. All of the efforts between two hospitals became fruitless and our son would slowly loose strength and pass away. He was dark haired, blue eyed and had all of the spirit of a son that I had dreamt he would have but he just didn't stay on this earth long enough.

These tragedies will be with me for life but can and do to this day make me a stronger more loving man than I ever have been. As I have taken the time to evaluate who I am, I review those things that have had the most influential impact on me. I think that we all do. When there have been hard times in life like deaths in the family or close friends, job losses, and divorce or any directly troublesome time, we see those as landmarks of the changes in our being, our self. As we stand on this earth as adults these things allow us to see the people that we are today and see our inner beings as a conglomerate of experience and learned behavior over time. This we can account for through psychology. Learned behavior can help us understand this but first we need a clearer idea as to how we retain the knowledge that is gathered and therefore a bit of the psychology and physiology of memory comes first.

There are three categories that draw attention here, the forming or encoding of a memory, the storage of the memory and the extraction of the information in bits or in full. With the encoding or forming of memory the details are kept longer in our minds based on the strength of the memory. Surly we remember more major impacts on our lives than simple, day to day ones. Short term memory usually lasts twenty to thirty seconds unlike long term memory that has a term of days, months and even years. Through our lives we are influenced by our environment and the things that happen to us within it. These experiences build memory, some long term, some short. The memories are built by excited neuro pathways using electrically stimulated nerves. During open cranial brain surgery in the 1960s, Dr. Wilder Penfield triggered through electro stimulation a memory that the patient had long thought to have forgotten. During these surgeries the patient is awake to make sure that the correct parts of the brain are worked on and that long term damage is not inflicted. These memories that are long lasting can at some points be stimulated through a linked memory, similar to my experience of smelling candles which triggered reflections of years past.

When the biochemistry of memory is examined many studies have been successful in their ventures finding that nerves have been found to be the clear and constant factor through all memory. When we are thinking of how chemicals can cause nerve stimulation there is a simple concept using two common electrolytes. When *potassium* and *sodium* switch places through the membrane of a nerve cell, an *action potential* takes place initiating a charge down the leg of the nerve to the next cell and so on. The potassium and sodium are key to the nerve cells ignition. When the nerve fires and starts a chain reaction this allows for stimulation of muscles giving us movement. That's why athletes drink things like Powerade because the electrolytes replace those that are released through sweat. If you ever look at the "P" on a Powerade bottle, turn it sideways and the wave you see is an action potential graph of a nerve cell. That is one way nerves get the electrical spark needed for activity and of course another would be the internal energy we have flowing through our bodies like that of the pace maker of the heart. I think that one thing that the concept of memory does not exaggerate on is the ability and process to store knowledge. Once we see something that becomes a memory, how exactly is it "stored" in our brains? This question I believe has been a challenge for years but truly to this day has no real answer but many possibilities. One of the possibilities is the concept of biological microchips. The technology of biochips or nanotechnologies and medicine, has emerged in the realms of molecular biology, immunology, biochemistry and other fields of study. The cells used are able to retain data through electrical stimulation within their proper environment. This concept alone can be implemented with the memory storage in the brain. The cells within the brain retain parts of the memory but also the links to the areas of the brain that maintain the remaining data. These areas are connected through nerve fibers and then accessed through the stimulation of the nerves themselves. The amount of data that can be stored at this first level of technology is massive and can only grow. So the memory potential we have within the brain cells for storage would also be on a large capacity. The birth of a memory is stimulated in an area of the brain triggering a nerve that in turn launches a chain reaction of linked nerves to other areas of the brain completing the compilation of a memory. When we have a very impressive experience the pathways linking the nerves are burned in stronger than when a less impressive one occurs this is called long term potential or LTP. LTP is a long lasting increase in neural excitability at synapses along a specific neural pathway. Imagine touching a hot surface for a brief second verses several seconds. The milder burn will leave a smaller scar that may even go away in time but the worse burn will leave a scar that most likely will be life long, the same with the neurological impressions of memory. Think of standing in your kitchen preparing to make a cake. All around you are the different things that you need from flour in the cupboard, milk in the refrigerator, and sugar in the jar or a mixer in the closet and so on. Each thing that you need is an individual item but put together becomes a process and a final outcome which is the cake itself. That is how a memory is stored in the brain. Several pieces can be at different locations in the brain but are brought together by the links of nerves. There is still much study to be done but the possibilities are becoming clearer.

Now that the concept of memory is understood we can look at the development of personality and behavior based on the learned facts we gather through life's experiences. Personality refers to an individual's unique structure of consistent behavioral traits. When a baby is born it has been said that times within the mother's womb have been turned into memories although the child has no developed language or specific labels for the experiences. It is clear that the infant will feel cold upon birth and that the tight wrap of a warm blanket is comforting so on that level the learning process has already begun. Even the familiar sound of a parent's voice can be recognized. This learning is beginning to develop the link between crying while cold and receiving a blanket resulting in an understanding of established process. In this early stage of learning it is clear that patterns can be developed but the question than, is what makes a "good" baby verses a "not so good" one? We have all said or at least heard people say "what a good baby" when referring to minimal crying or fussing. When a baby is smiling a lot or not displaying a cranky attitude, we call it "good". The answer may go back to one or all of three places biological, psychological and or spiritual.

In the case of genetics several scientists have based their findings on the personality consistencies of identical twins.

Hans Eysenck had studied twins and found that raised separate or together many identical characteristics were evident. The more the studies have taken place over time, the more it is clear that genetic code assists in placing a baseline for personality but does not immediately upon birth reflect individual personality traits. Though it can be said that genetics cause an influence in directions for personality, the individualism taking place before personality development is yet to be deciphered. The deeper we go into the earliest stages of infant growth we can ask if it is possible that a spirit based personality already exists. At birth the "good" baby clearly is displaying personality characteristics altogether different from those of more fussy babies. Many times it can be directed to an upset stomach, cramping, teething or other physical condition happening, other times it cannot. At this point in time there is no comprehensible biological theory of personality. We have to ask ourselves if genetics represents a portion of our personality development than where in the genetic code does it lye? The deeper the study of genetics takes us the more individual characteristics are identifiable in genetic code. It has been found that hair and eye color can be detected so surly the brain functionality in terms of personality could also be detectable on a cellular level. The segment of the genetic structure that is responsible for these changes must be in the growth structure of the brain, furthermore than we would need to ask how a portion of the brain functions more or less in order to produce an individual personality trait. One possibility is a heightened neurological activity in one or more portions of the brain that is responsible for certain behavior. For the most part though, biological concepts don't provide a systematic overview of how they govern personality development. The feasibility of genetic personality traits is evident with the study of twins after development but other options as well as the earliest stages can still be explored. So now at this point we have the first option of genetics, which is a tangible standpoint but holds a lot of mysterious quarks leading us to the psychological points of view.

Psychology has developed concepts through the years and primarily just approved upon them as more studies have been done. The difficult thing to prove in any case is an intangible object. In this matter the personality is exactly that.

The more we accumulate information through all possible sources the more we see that some conclusions in life are made by the heart. Our inner feelings tell us what is right and wrong or what seems to be more feasible even though one answer may be more tangible than the other. The efforts in this book are to put facts and theory together and than allow the reader to make a decision by themselves. To get a clearer picture of psychology's view of personality we need to once again feel our way through. Here are some more aspects to behavior and psychological individualism.

Through the years several theorists have made major impacts on the psychology of personality and behavior. Sigmund Freud emphasized on the fixation or progress through psychosexual stages and experiences in early childhood that can have long lasting effects on adult personality. B.F. Skinner focused on personality evolving gradual over the life span specifically responses to stimulus and reinforcement. Carl Rogers studied children that if receiving unconditional love seem to have less need to be defensive and that they develop more accurate self concepts. Hans Eysnick emphasized on the unfolding of genetic blueprints as the person matures and how inherited predispositions interact with learning experiences. These great minds in the field of psychology have given us a wonderful and consistent manner in the understanding of personality. All of the students funneling through colleges across the country and even the world study the findings of these great minds. These formats allow us to see how as time goes on, we as human beings develop mannerisms, thought processes, concepts and behaviors all through the interaction with our environments and the people within them. Our influences from a day to day exposure give us perceptions of what we see happening around us and compares that to what is *actually* happening around us. Our perceptions drive us to conclusions sometimes fast and sometimes slow. With the cultivation of experience we also have something more that gives us a push in certain directions, the conscience. We all have been in positions in our lives that we have a *feeling* about an instance. A certain rush of energy that makes us decide on a point of view without much preparation or thinking. When we know something is wrong we feel it inside. This leads us into the theories of another great mind in psychology of self, Carl Jung. His ventures in psychiatry lead him to become world-famous but also controversial, the first modern psychiatrist to recognize that the human psyche is "by nature religious". He proclaimed himself a "healer of the soul" and reached deep within himself as well as his patients. He recognized two "lives" an outer and an inner as the natural state of realized humanity and believed he was earth rooted but spiritually centered. I know when I began to explore this, time after time I had to ask myself how I see this fitting into myself personally. How can these theories fit into the way that I have understood my individual self. Jung's theories have helped me see an aspect of personality that fits more than many others that I have studied. The questions we ask about the voices of conscience and the deep inside feeling of right and wrong can be closer to having answers with these views. But again the plan is to understand a complete balance of body, mind and spirit that will allow us to grasp the understanding of our individual self.

Jung believed in individuation, a coming to self hood, believing in a natural law that man becomes to recognize the whole being that he is and has become including inner soul and outer body. In this process the human being recognizes itself as both material and spiritual, conscious and unconscious. That the conscious mind spends its time in two floors of a six story building and that the unconscious mind explores the remaining floors. While we are at rest or sleeping our subconscious being attempts to relay information to the conscious being through dreams and ideas. The first level we come across in the unconscious is what Jung called the shadow. These are the parts of ourselves we don't understand or like in ways. We display these outwardly towards others reflecting in them characteristics that we don't like. Our inner demons have plagued us from birth and I think I can state that literally. From the very beginning we start our personal evaluations by comparing ourselves to those around us and what we think we would like to be. The more our opinions develop and take up room in our secret garden our shadow begins to grow and is fed from this manifestation. I personally can trace some of these back to when I was very young, seeing that I started to build this darkness as a result of my experiences. Although this concept sounds similar to the tradition of learned behavior through influence this is uniquely clearer in the end, you'll see. We have the opportunity to begin this understanding of the shadow when we do self inventories. While mulling around in our inner reflection we see the dark spots of our shadow and then can identify them and further clarify their origins. Jung recognized this within himself and the challenges it produced.

> *"You may shake your head incredulously when I tell you that I hardly have been able to form the concept of the shadow had not its existence become one of my greatest experiences, not just in regard to other people but with regard to myself....*
>
> *My shadow is indeed so huge that I could not possibly overlook it in the plan of my life; in fact I had to see it as an essential part of my personality, accept the consequences of this realization, and take responsibility for them. Many bitter circumstances have forced me to see that though the sin that one has committed or is can be regretted, it is not*

cancelled out. I don't believe in the tiger who was finally
converted to vegetarianism and ate only apples"

"Recognizing the shadow is what I call the apprentiship.
But making out the anima is what I call the masterpiece
which not many bring off."

-Carl Jung

It is with the understanding of the shadow that we can
move on in a more clear maintenance of ourselves. I have spent
a lot of time in many unfortunate situations forcing myself to
go into these places within to understand my inner fears and
the reasons why I felt the way that I did. The more time I spend
doing these inventories of my shadow the more things that were
hidden away for years would come to surface. Not only did I
face things that I knew were there I also stumbled upon things
that I didn't. The path of the individuation process leads to an
inner growth that emerges into our consciousness providing
us with a deeper understanding and a fuller, more mature
personality. Our personality is what we use to display what we
feel inside based on our conclusions derived from a compilation
of our conscious and unconscious. If the feelings within
reflect a completeness between the two than a comfortable
understanding of our world around us will be displayed through
our actions and the way we carry ourselves. Using this method
of self inventory we can begin to see what it is exactly that has
structured our personality. I use this inventorying as often as
I have significant changes in my life and even randomly we can
ask ourselves *how am I doing? Anything new?* As if talking to an
old friend.

The more time I have spent breaking this all down, I don't
think the benefit is to identify the personality of long ago but
to recognize who we are today. For each of us this venture is to
find a way to come closer to the inner being that exists within
each of us and then to learn of its origin. This inner being is the
energy within that joins our physical self, one living and dying

and one that lives eternally. As we become older and we have the opportunities to stop and listen to the world around us and look within ourselves we will be able to understand who we are today. My biggest challenge to this very dawning was coming to a point where I could say that I felt good with who I am. I needed to become good for myself before I could ever be worth anything to those I loved the most. To do this I had to put away those things that smothered me, a past that I could and would finally shut the door on. I could not move on with feelings of guilt hanging over my shoulder. These things had to be faced and finished once and for all.   Once that was done I had to work on forgiveness. Not becoming weak or foolish by allowing those that hurt me to do it again but to strategically place those issues where they belonged. I read something somewhere that helped me understand the meaning of forgiveness. It was not the simplicity of turning the other cheek, or the relentless beating down but the recognition of those that I have hurt and that have hurt me, to understand clearly those issues and then put them in the past to let go and to move forward in my life. That point of understanding gave me a feeling of freeness and made me excited to look to God and open my heart, mind and soul to his will. Once we have a clear picture of our self we then can filter the outer opinions of who we are and further evaluate our needs to build on or take away certain characteristics. There will always be input from the world whether we like it or not. Some will be valuable pieces of information and others maybe not be but if we are not open to our surroundings and the existence around us we will loose many gifts and pass on the chance to enjoy Gods creations. The living, pumping and dynamic world in which we live in is beating like a heart constantly. An energy that is not only within us but circulating around us flooding our planes with information. It is up to us to pay close attention to it and extract all of the knowledge that is given to us either consciously or unconsciously. Our personalities will always be a mystery, not a book or a voice will answer the questions we have to completeness. Our individuality is within ourselves and up to us to unlock it using all of the tools we gather through our lives. Furthermore we have the gifts of spirit and intuition that can guide us along the way. It is the access to that guide that can be for most quite a troublesome task. But it is there, as certain as the cloths we wear or the sky above and there are secrets to that energy that if we choose to confront them we can thrive off of the wonderful world we live in. So now there are things to move into and look at as potential answers to the origins of spirit, the identity of the energy around us and the proof that not only is the physical body and the personality within it a miracle of God but the world and universe in which it all connects to is also.

Section Three

The search for Understanding

*A*fter reading the first section of this book I wanted the readers to have a clearer understanding of the unique intricacies of the human body. It is such an amazing machine and the little details of function are so delicate but durable that human existence simply mutating from a pond is not an option. The details are too specific, engineered understanding at its best today cannot come close to the creative mind of our God. The brain itself, such a wonderful gift and it holds such massive potential that even the greatest thinkers of history have not breeched its capabilities. Our heart beats with full strides of strength and resilience all on an invisible battery pack giving us more time to live a life here on earth. Our bodies being such a miracle are built for use and study, for understanding and function. We have been given a great opportunity and a tool to do it with, a vessel in which we can travel to the lengths of earth and beyond to explore life around us. Right where you sit, stand, walk, run or lie on the ground, you are surrounded by active miracles and vibrating energy. You are aglow with spirit waiting to be molded, fed and accessed. As special and unique as you are, as so individual in mind and body as you clearly have become, you are also an energy as different as the colors of life around you. Your personalities have developed over the years of your travels day to day and night after night. With each experience we have molded into the beings that we are today but not hardened like a clay pot in a kiln. We are still soft enough to manipulate and reshape our inner and outer beings. We can yet do so many amazing things with the world and all of those spirits and energies around us. All we have to do is recognize its potential and its name and reach out with blinders flung to the wind and open our minds and hearts to the brilliance and exuberance of the universe and the Holy Spirit that encompasses it all. Today is the day, here and now is the time. We have a chance to harness and embrace this life while we are still here. We are all linked together by a powerful yet peaceful tie. A lanyard of togetherness comprised of love, energy, wisdom and strength. This is your opportunity to make one of the most influential changes in your life. This date, today's date, say it to yourself right now, month, day and year. This is the first time in all of your existence that you are in this moment in time and the only chance you will ever have for the remainder of your life to see this day. Do something that you will never forget. Before you put your head on your pillow to say goodnight do something that will make this day remain permanently special. Here, Now, This is the time........ This is *your* time!

Levels

*L*evels are the separate platforms in the depths of understanding consciousness and sub-consciousness. Through these levels we can see more clearly the way that the energies around and within can be seen influencing our lives. From the general level of operating day to day through routine thought process to the complete separation of spirit and body, we are functioning on several plains of consciousness. We are approached and influenced by the energies around us in the form of feelings, ideas, emotions, directions and many other stimuli and it is up to us to recognize them and determine on what level and category they fall into. We all have been asked to do something at work or at home by bosses, colleagues, family, friends or even strangers. We build the request by compiling facts through thought process that are happening on a first level of consciousness. If we need to ponder on or learn a piece of the information, we find that on a secondary level along with the *free will* used to determine what we will do with the formulated information. REM sleep and types of hypnosis that *access* sub-conscious are in a third level and the fourth and fifth levels are the subconscious influence and the separation of spirit and body.

If we think of life and the energies around us we can compare it to coming into a house for the first time. We enter from a vast exterior of world and universe and in through a door of first level consciousness. At this level things are routine and recognizable but functional and comfortable. As we enter into the house we admire the things within and make evaluations based on the feelings we have when we sit in the chairs or walk through the rooms. With those influences we are able to determine if we would like to continue and if the first blush of the house is safe or not. The *feel* of the house becomes our conscience and the energy input we receive from around us becomes our guide. As we continue deeper into the house we look into closets and cupboards, we open drawers and try on cloths and we *think* of what we can do with our new things. Our ideas begin to flow and the modifications we would like to make stir curiosity, character and creativity. Our inner energies drive us to new highs through the influence of those around us and we become at home with our new chateau. As our walk through our home continues we find things that we don't like and things that we do but realize that it is up to us to make our new house truly a home so we change the things that we can and accept those things that we cannot. Our connection to the energy around us helps us through our home and the more in touch we are with them the more solitude we find. As the tour ends and our lives come to a close, we walk from the back door and into the lush, pure and loving backyard of the vast universe in which we came. This is what we have in front of us and the levels of consciousness that we develop the most to associate with these energies will help us live a great life. There are many people and examples that fall into these levels and the more detail we go into each one, the clearer it will be as to how each level works for us. The further these are understood we will see how these energies can act for or even against us. Each level has an energy that works mostly within it. Just like the instincts of animals are drawing from the energy that directs predetermined performance. The trees, grass and all things growing upward are actually growing outward, drawn to an energy that encircles the earth. We on the other hand operate on a much more intelligent and intricate energy. One that is saturated with knowledge and information, nourished with artistic creation and delightful dance steps, energies that have fortified through years of experience and toil but resulted in character and strength. These energies have guided leaders through history, the brushes of great artists, the tools of sculptors, the steps of creators and clearly the hearts of those we love and that love us in return. The energy of the Holy Spirit guided Jesus Christ through his many teachings and flowed deep and strong in the performing of miracles. The same energy that has been here since the beginning of time remains here still and all around and within us.

The first level is one of the most commonly used places of our daily activity. The step by step routines that do not take a lot of contemplation happen here. As time goes on and we develop a memory of specific things that we access the most like brushing our teeth, walking down the hallway or out the door or simply going to the bathroom, we do not need to think much when doing them. We go through our day functioning in this state of consciousness on an even keel for the most part with not a lot of need to deviate. The more we come into a daily pathway of routine circumstance, the more time we spend in this level. Some times we find ourselves in our jobs not escaping from the rigors of day to day conditioning and seeing the day come to an end with no deviance at all. We get up when the alarm goes off, we start the coffee pot or maybe have one that starts automatically so we make sure we are in a routine, go to the bathroom and look into a mirror reflecting into a face that we do not take the time to see, get dressed in pre laid out cloths, go off to work driving the same route, do our non-stimulating jobs, return from work, finish the day, set the alarm and hit the hay. Another day has come to an end but the level we started in had stayed the same for just about the whole day. We never really left home. This level of consciousness allows us to be consistent with less fluctuation but truly becomes a bit grey in time. This level is a must although, because we cannot start any project without a launching pad for ideas. Our days have routine so that we have an even plane to begin our challenges and have an understanding of beginning. We gather facts in this state and develop perceptions using pre-learned information. From our stimuli in the environments we are in through the day and night we make associations continuously and for the most part don't even realize it. When so many things are happening around us we simply choose what we allow through the filter and use only a small percent of our worlds. Even when we see something that is new or different we dismiss it and don't even allow for the level of consciousness that contributes to imagination to open up. There are energies to be received continuously, seen and unseen all around us but our filters deny them and we carry on in our tunnel. Looking around as we step from the bus, we view our surroundings to make sure we don't run into anyone and that we go in the right direction but in order to do just that, thousands of action potentials are taking place through the nerve pathways in our bodies and brains. Even the littlest things are miracles. This level sets the standard for imagination and ideas with the brick base structure of understanding. This is the level in which our senses have the ability to give us information at high speeds, some to process and discharge and others to feed intuition for further evaluation. When we receive stimuli from our outside world we can either stay in level one and use what is necessary for day to day operation, or dissect it a little bit and take ourselves into another level for evaluation and manipulation. Our bodies rely on level one to do the functions that we need no attention for. After enough time we should be able to move our limbs, eat, recognize, associate, breath and calculate without any attention at all. It is in this state though that we do not take the time to look deeper at the things happening around us. Not just the bus, but the people on the bus. Not just the coffee, but who poured it for you. Not only the walk to work, but the wonderful things around you walk along the way. Not just the door that you open to go into work, but the person you held it for as you let them pass. The desire to bring our attention to the details around us, if even just for a second, takes us into a different level in which we *think* of what we are seeing and feeling not just dismissing it along the way as part of the trip. We can think of the first level of more of a physiological or bodily state. A place where a lot of the things we do are derived from memory and learned behavior. When we use our senses to bring the world around us into a thought rather than an object, we open ourselves to the energies around us that have so much to offer. *There is solace in routine but the most wonderful gifts are left unseen.* Being awake in this level now can open the doors to a secondary level, one of ideas and evaluations and of creation and color. There is a specific route that is taken from the open door of level one all the way to the connection to the most powerful energies around us. At the point of first levels we can open our minds to the opportunity of advancement into other levels, but cannot move on without a place to start.

This leads us into the second level. At this point we have the ability to venture out into the fascinating world and universe God gave us. This is the first blush at the true energy potential within and our ability to communicate and access the energy without. At the second level we have feelings, emotions, conscience, day dreaming, inner energy movements and the trading of vibrations between us and others. It is here that we have taken off the blinders and found that there is truly more to this life and world than we see in our level one consciousness. At level two our awareness begins to bloom into a splendid and unique display of individuality that truly becomes who we are. The learned methods of activity slide a door open to the colorful romance of life as God intended us to see, but not on a physical standard, an emotional connection to the spirit of all living things. It communicates to us as we allow it to speak and listen to the wisdom it provides. In this state of awareness we have the stir of creation and loss of self doubt. We inherit the willingness to let go of the past which will out fashion the guilt of flat conscious living. Here is the birth of *free will* and the beginning of formed character combining sub-consciousness with awakeness and compiling a recipe for greatness and satisfaction. We come across events in our lives that we choose to evaluate or dismiss based on feelings. A feeling is not just a physical reaction to a stimulus but the reaching of our spiritual self to our conscious state maneuvering us based on our stability with the Holy Spirit. Surely we all have had the feeling of right and wrong virtually immediately when confronted with a situation. When our physical bodies feel heart ache, pain or joy, we relate it to the actual feelings within the body. Those muscles and tissues are affected by the chemicals released by the brain, the hub of electrical circuitry, and cause the actual physical feeling we feel. So in essence heart ache is actual physical discomfort. The start of that feeling though comes from the brains reception of energetic impulse which comes from our internal conscience directed by our outwardly connected spirit. So though the body reacts in a physical manner, it is the energy that initiates the reaction. These feelings that we relate to right and wrong are also connected to conscience. Surly we have had what we call angels and demons on our shoulders influencing our decisions or more specifically our free will. Though a large part of learned experience plays a major role in the conditioning of free will, the conscience is the pathway from the spirit and works close with our physical self nurturing the will to do right. We are all set on this earth on our own free will which gives us the opportunity to make decisions based on how we feel inside and from the experiences we have had in the past. Our free will cannot be developed without a deeper more mature understanding of individuality through self recognition. The more our complete self is satisfied, the more functional our free will becomes to assist us with our lives. Carl Jung believed that man needed to become his complete self in order to live whole. This is why back in the section on psychology, it is necessary to confront and deal with our shadows in order to carry on in our life investment.

Our willingness to face the intricacies of our dislikes and our faults will shape our platform for greater self work in the future. The difficulty for some people to make the right decisions is in direct relation to their connection to their subconscious and the development of free will. The matter being viewed by a person that has experienced negativity from making the bad choice and fortifies positiveness by pursuing the right path will enforce the conscience for future matters. The development of solid free will and the outcomes from the decisions made by free will all come down to the connection between the level one inner energy (consciousness) and level two and three energy (sub-consciousness) and the outer energy (the spirit around us). All must link together fluently in order to have positive results from choices made by free will. Our conscience has allowed for a base point of that development and the more consistency there is in positive efforts, the more fortified and balanced the results will be. When the results are positive, the universe attracts the results and the return is positive in the future. This level of consciousness opens the connection to so much more than we realize. This is the chance to generate a heightened potential and a womb for knowledge, strength and wisdom.

Further into the second level we have creativity and day dreaming. We are taking ourselves out of the day to day routine just enough to open our minds to the possibilities of outer influence. When we day dream we are allowing ourselves to think more intensely on an idea at hand. When we are willing to breathe just enough to pursue creativity we can open our conscious being to a deeper potential. Our ideas that come to us are through the increase in neurological activity going on in our brains. When we look at the fMRI of a person that is day dreaming there is an increase in the strength of energy released through many lobes of the brain. With this increase comes not only the ability to access memories or long hidden thoughts but also new and unidentified ideas. The energy within us increases when we allow for new outside influence to join with our existing being. I'm sure we have had the experience of thinking about a topic and one or several answers or concepts come to mind. Some we may have already used and others that may have never *consciously* crossed our minds before. We are using our willingness to access our sub-conscious and feed from the outer energy. One of the greatest things we can offer this world is a well maintained and loving individualism. Our creative mind gives us just that chance by giving ourselves the opportunity to dream. When we take the time to look around us and open up to possibility, the world in which we live in provides gifts through visuals, sounds, smells and vibrations that can then stimulate our creative minds. According to psychology we have sudden bursts of insight and imagination and Robert Weisberg called it the *aha! Myth*. Undeniably creative bursts do occur (Feldman 1988). Creative achievements are surly developed from lots of long term thinking and hard work but even on those planes we find some of our biggest breakthroughs come when we least expect it.

It seems that at this point we have such an enormous opportunity to get closer to the wonders of our universe and that if we take advantage of it we can truly make it work for us and even more so it becomes a reciprocation of positive energy. So here, at level two, we are becoming more awake to the energies and are finding out how it is influencing even the simplest of activities. We are learning to recognize it and feeling its potential through our openness. When I first attended an Alcoholics Anonymous meeting, I found myself unsure as to what the purpose of the steps was. As the meeting progressed it made sense to me that the steps were a lead into a much greater find. When we were finished with the meeting we all stood and held hands in a big circle and closed by reciting The Lords Prayer. Later in the months of attendance I realized that the saying of the prayer, even though many did not believe directly in God, it was a lead into a relationship with him that was to take place down the road. By just saying the Lords Prayer as a group we were unknowingly gathering in Gods name and praying together for the strength of sobriety. It was the little piece that sparked the fire of Love and Respect for our God not only as we knew him but for the wonderful God he is. The level we are in at this stage is also the launching platform for greater things and the joining of spirit and energy within us.

We have the best chance to access these capabilities when we are in this zone of being awake and quiet, one of openness and willingness to more than what we are. We can use tools available to get even closer to these energies. One of these tools is meditation. Meditation allows us to come to a deeper quietness to our surroundings and closer to hearing the messages from our sub-conscious. Through this tool we are able to focus even more specifically on *hearing* what we are being told and *feeling* the vibrations from the world around us. Using meditation broadens even more the portal between the universe, our world and its energies and all of our levels of consciousness. Carl Jung had enjoyed his quiet time so much that he built a house just for the advantage of solitude. He believed that with the busy activity of living we cannot hear the message of spirit. I enjoy closing my eyes in public places and just thinking of the people around me. I don't think of them in a physical way but in their energy or spirit form. If you try this you will begin to feel different energies from people without even knowing what they look like. I imagine the strength of energy being depicted in how bright they glow and scurry about or calmly enjoy their walk. If you relax enough to open your mind to this, you will feel just what I'm telling you. You can try this anywhere, on a bus, at an event, a mall but one of the best places is a park. In the park people are surrounded by the energy in all living things and the glow seems brighter. In a park people are also usually having a good time which heightens the level of energy even more, feeding off of positivity all around them. This exercise allows you to not only stop and be quiet for a bit but also recognize that there is so much more going on around us than we realize.

Another tool used for relaxation for the mind and body is meditation. Meditation refers to a family of practices that train attention and heighten awareness allowing for the body and mind to become under better control. Yoga, Zen and Transidental Meditation all come from Eastern religions but it has been used through out history as a tool to simply bring ourselves to a relaxed state of body and mind. Although most people in the Western part of the world don't relate meditation to religious factors, the bible refers to it when pursuing connection with the Holy Spirit. The bible describes methods of thought and meditation to come closer to receiving the energy of the spirit of God. We can use this as a tool when we need to come down from a busy state or need to simply relax.

There are two main types of meditation that we can go over in this section, Concentrative and Mindfulness Meditations. The first is concentrative, when we put our focus on an image or a sound to bring our mind to a more central point and allow for a higher clarity. The easiest way to do this would be to focus directly on your breathing; professionals in this field believe that there is a close tie between breath control and the pace of the mind. By concentrating on slowing our breathing to a nice, slow and even pace, the minds speed will also slow and become leveled. Once the mind is calm and relaxed, the energy around us has the opportunity to enter and be absorbed into our consciousness. This falls into the same idea of day dreaming about a specific thing that would also allow for you to come to a steady and mellow state of mind. The idea is to totally bring your mind away from the chaos of the busy day and the distractions around you and be available for incoming vibrations. You can use anything that will allow you to take the focus from the world around you to a center point in your mind. You may even use the sound of slow and steady waves coming to the shore or the soft sounds of a wind chime. Another type of meditation is mindfulness. With this type of meditation you will bring yourself to a one way street of stimulus. Let the feelings, images, sounds, smells, sensations and vibrations funnel through your mind but choose not to interact with them. Just simply let these things free fall through the windows of your mind and watch and listen to each and every one of them. The key here is how you focus not necessarily what you're focusing on. What is more important is the quality of awareness that you bring to each moment. There are two kinds of mindful meditation – formal and informal. One good example of formal would be yoga where participants slowly move from one position to another concentrating on their breathing and posture. Breathing is the tool of transition from a state of stress to one of relaxation and tranquility. During this state of meditation, you will find your body at rest and allowing the energy around you to come and be received. At the same time that the body rests, the mind becomes more aware of the input from around you and will much more vividly display its images. During these states of proper and deep meditation there are several things happening physically that can assist with then relaxation process. There is a fall in metabolic rate indicating a drop in oxygen intake. The reduced intake has come down in studies as much as twenty percent which is below the level of deep sleep. The heart rate and the breathing rates decrease giving the body an opportunity for true relaxation. The electrical current resistance of the skin also decreases which tells us that the muscles are relaxing to the point of major a reduction in energy retention. It is also found that through meditation we learn to access the relaxation response which controls the way we respond to negative stimulus and stress.

Electroencephalograms show that there is a reduction is faster paced rhythms of the brain during meditation showing a wave reflecting a much more relaxed pace. There have also been findings of total relaxation that is fuller and more productive than trance and deep sleep. Again the point with these exercises is to get ourselves to the point of complete relaxation giving us the chance to listen and receive the energy around us. Meditation in an all around manner has been found to be one of the best ways for the body to come to a state of healing. When the body reduces its stress levels, not only are the muscles relaxing but the chemicals in the body that can be harmful when over secreted are reducing. More towards the end of this book I have some easy methods for you to use to meditate that have been shown to work within days of practice.

Approaching level three we are getting deeper into the realm of sub-consciousness. At this point we would be in dream sleep or random eye movement (REM) sleep. The eye movement usually comes from the active role we are playing in our dreams where we are actually looking around. The deeper we are in this sleep, the more vivid are active the dreams will be. At this stage we are at the will of our sub-conscious the most. For years psychologists have tried to interpret dreams and help us understand more of the strange meaning behind some of those experiences. We all have had some very unique and tranquil dreams and of course some absolutely off the wall dingers that don't seem to have any connection to our lives what so ever. Sigmund Freud and Carl Jung would talk to each other explaining their dreams trying to find meaning to them and would each allow the other to try to interpret them. Jung believed that dreams are a way for the sub-conscious to send messages to the conscious self through symbols or signs of sorts. When we are in this state of relaxation, we are even deeper than most meditation and are much more susceptible to the input from our sub-conscious energy. A lot of people, including myself, will take a note pad and put it by my bedside to keep track of the dreams that I have. If you can imagine your sub-conscious being like an excited little child coming to wake you constantly on Christmas morning, than you can see the how it is necessary to answer the child and either send them back to bed or get up and open presents. When our sub-conscious is very active and receiving messages for us to be aware of, it is necessary to pay attention to what is being sent and receive them as best we can.

Dreams have been a curious thing for many years. Psychology has made a valiant effort to decipher them and find some consistent pattern as to their meaning but to this day we have not been able to thoroughly put them to paper. A study by Calvin Hall was done in the 1960's that evaluated over 10,000 dreams and built a list of many consistencies that people recall all around the world. According to Hall dreams seem to stay centered on sources of internal conflicts and are self centered, dreaming about themselves. Some of the most common are of being chased or pursued but not physically injured; some are of sexual nature and of falling or being on the verge of falling. This links to the unrest of the sub-conscious reaching to resolve pent up issues that we need to address in our daily lives. Our dreams seem mostly to reflect what is going on in our lives and the current time and place that our most influential experiences are taking place. Studies also show that people dream a lot of those things that would be better off forgotten. When we try to put away influential instances that are unresolved, the sub-conscious tries to offer a reminder of things left undone. So it seems that those things that we try to suppress during our days make an appearance in our dreams at night. Although many people in our part of the world dismiss dreams as meandering thoughts and useless information, other cultures see them as sources of information about oneself, or messages about our lives or even a link to the spiritual world. Australian Aborigines believe dreaming is the focal point of existence and directly effects their way of life and their relationship to the spiritual world around them. People in some cultures also believe that dreams provide information about the future. This is also reflected in the experiences of Edgar Cayce that follows further in this book. Dream patterns show a direct relation also to the culture of the people and the location of the world that they live in. The dreams of people in parts of the world that are in common conflict have reflected dreams that are connected to that and the difficulties that a society at war presents. The messages that are being sent at any stage of cultural outlay are that there is communication happening between our sub-conscious and conscious levels of our lives. One thing that has been found through all dream studies is that the person remains in an episode directly including themselves. Our dreams are using our internal issues and conflicts to further resolve them. Carl Jung believed that in this state of dreaming certain symbols may reflect the message and that if other people dream of the same symbol that they are connected in the same issue although may not realize it in a conscious state. The links between the energies within and around us are at constant attempt and dreams are just another way that these can be heard.

Other theorists, such as Rosalind Cartwright, have suggested that dreams are a way for us to work through everyday problems and emotional issues. She believes that a cognitive, problem solving view exists between waking and sleeping thought. We engage in creative thinking because dreams are not restrained by logic or realism. Deeper than we can ask ourselves where the answers to these issues come from. Not only do we dream of the unresolved or conflicting issue we also come up, at times, with a solution to the problem. This goes back to the connection between the sub-conscious and the energies around us including the Holy Spirit. Sigmund Freud said that "(Dreams are) the royal road to the unconscious." We have the ability to extract information from the universe around and beyond us with the willingness to accept it as real. By relaxing ourselves to the point of release from conscious bonds we are allowing for the messages from our unconscious to flow into our waking mind. When this concept is considered there are several influences that can derail the messages being sent through dreams. It is very important to be aware of what is happening during our dream state and no matter how bizarre the dreams may be an evaluation of them allows for a possible solution to an issue at hand. Documenting those episodes is important so we don't forget what was passed to us.

Another great thing to use can be music created for the use of meditation. For many years the theory that certain sound pitches and levels can be a very powerful meditation tool. Robert Gass has created a cd that is focused on the levels and structures of sound that can directly calm the energy within. The objective with this would be to find, as specifically as possible, a tone that would sooth the spirit energy the most. Through experiment and study the result is a fascinating find and can most certainly do exactly that. If we think of electrical towers and the sound that is being released by the mass energy traveling through their tentacles of wire, we can imagine that even on small basis energy emits sound. Though the humming of the energy may be very light and perhaps so delicate that the human ears cannot pick it up, the energy within can. The spirit energy that is within had to come from a source and most likely that source contains many more than one energy which would emit a much more clear and definable sound vibration. This sound, if mimicked on earth, may instantly calm our spirit energy by exposing ourselves to its tones. Many specialists, theorists and imaginers have believed that music or sound structures can deeply affect the spirit and therefore can be a wonderful piece to our settling of our restless energies.

The point to all of this, whether it is day dreaming, meditation, sleep study and dreams themselves, trances, hypnosis or any other method of relaxation, is to see how we can listen the clearest to the energy around and within us. We can see already that information can be passed from one person to another through the concept of thought forms so if we can accept the idea of information being available in the world around us in this state than we can further see how we can receive it.

Even deeper than dream sleep is the tool of hypnosis. If the point of the messages or information from the energies around us is to be received and acknowledged than the deeper we can go into a state of calmness and willingness is the objective. There have been many theories developed to explain hypnosis but it is still for the most part not understood. One is that the person is put into a deep state of consciousness called a *hypnotic trance*. Despite the doubts of the validity of hypnosis, many theorists maintain that hypnotic effects are due to a state of mind that cannot be faked or role played. The most capable study results are from brain activity tests during hypnosis that show the same waves and findings as if the person was in a hallucination state. This can explain if the person is able to dismiss pain response during hypnosis. I don't want to go too far with this topic because it is not really something that we can use in a daily manner to help us greet the energy we are seeking. This is just one more way that a person can get to a state of relaxation that can more sufficiently allow for the monitoring of the spirit base around us. Again the objective is to get ourselves to the point in which we can stop and feel, receive and enjoy the gifts that God has offered us through the Holy Spirit. We need to be able to control our minds energy and our body's hyperactivity by putting ourselves in a released state of mind giving up the stress and chaos of the world in which we live.

Edgar Cayce, the well known prophet, would have messages of all sorts come through him during deep sleep and trances that were very vivid and many were of future events that were later proven to be true. Cayce was able to find a level of trance that would allow him access to not only valuable information but what seemed to be messages referring to future events. In the beginning Cayce found himself with recipes for medical treatments that actually worked but had no past relation to any of the pharmacology or health care fields. These messages would come to him while in a sleep like state and in the form of statements as if being spoken to.

Cayce, ever since he was a boy, was able to do some amazing things. His talents started out to be questionable due to the magnitude of his memory and the manners in which he would feed it. But more than just his memory, his ability to tell the future and his access to knowledge that surly was beyond typical luck or just trickery. If we were to think of someone that had these abilities, we think of an old woman hovering over a crystal ball dressed as a gypsy or a mysterious palm reader on a dark street with a foggy alley. But through the years several people of professional status have come forth with an ability to see things that are beyond human thinking with true character and sincere direction. Some over time have acted as if this talent was more of a burden than anything else and would trade it for a seemingly regular life. In exchange for normalcy Edgar Cayce became more than just a psychic of types, he became an American Prophet. A man that became so great at his skill to channel these experiences into positive result that he was seen as truly gifted and blessed.

To further dissect how this talent could be functional, we would need to look at the ways that doing such a thing would be possible. One example would be for one to be able to read another persons mind. To be able to go into and receive a wave of thought that would be projected outward in a manner that would be like a radio wave of sorts. Let's think of the thought process again. When we create thought in our mind we access several parts of the brain through nerve pathways using electrical stimulation. These areas of the brain compile the knowledge that each section maintains and at the end of the linked pathways is a compilation of learned facts becoming a complete thought. During this whole process our brains are exuding energy that is generated during the process and is readable through electroencephalograms. This energy also could be picked up using a device similar to the amprobe that I explained earlier to detect energy around wire. In this case the other person is picking these waves up and is processing the thought and developing an image in their own minds. The receiving person draws the energy from the released thought;

it would have to be done with a clear and focused mind and attentive subconscious. A term used in esoteric psychology and metaphysics for the energy released during thinking is called a *thought form*. From this point of view thoughts become things, non-physical energy configurations. At this point the energy is projected into a form outside of the body when the efforts to develop the thought by the initiated person are strong and specific. The thoughts we construct at this point become more receptive the stronger it is and the more effort we put into the idea. So the concept of mind reading could be visualized as a calculable process. The person that is receiving the energy that is released may not be doing the majority of the work at all but just simply able to train their mind in a way that allows for incoming energy to be processed into material. If we think of the reception and the subconscious mind being the behind the scene key grips than the relaying of the data is through communication of the physical, conscious self. In essence this is energy receiving energy, one drawn to the other. Under this light the idea of mind reading becomes less of a mystery and more of a scientific advantage. This is then one way it may be possible for this information to be received.

Perhaps another way would be through the direct delivery of information through spiritual entities.

Edgar Cayce had been able to do some amazing things and these are just a couple ways that this information could have been channeled. At this first blush we will go into more of the experiences of Cayce himself. Through his time as a boy, Cayce found that he could retain vast amounts of knowledge by placing his head on books. I know in school we would joke about getting the information by napping on our books using osmosis, but in the matter of Edgar Cayce something else was happening. It wasn't just as simple as laying on a book I don't think. There is always something more to these things. Though this seemed to be a hoax being played on family and teachers, it later was clear that the information was truly becoming retained and that not only could young Edgar answer question in reference to the data, he was also able to give specific locations from within the book that the words were located. So the information was being retained but if we look at the processes of retention discussed earlier, we can see that there would need to be a source sending the energy in order for Cayce to receive it. The book itself cannot produce it. The other option would be that Cayce's sub-conscious could leave him far enough to see the information and bring it back or that it was being delivered by other energies all together. In either way the books pages were still being planted into Cayce's mind for him. The more that Cayce practiced this he was able to carry on excelling in school by using his new found talents. As time had gone on, a young Cayce found himself wanting to be a preacher, quoting and enjoying his favorite book of all, the bible. The chapters of the bible became a hidden treasure of knowledge and enjoyment for him and as time would pass he would use his love for the bible to teach Sunday school. Edgar also organized a local chapter of Christian endover, a world wide interdenominational outreach program from the 1880's. Edgar clearly found a solace in Christianity and would use his talents to further his studies of the bible and his faith. It wasn't the specific religion that captured his interest but the Christian hood alone that drew him close. Surely Edgar had no idea how his close relationship with God would contribute to his talents and advance his career and popularity. The years passing would bring Cayce to a stronger more developed sense of what his capabilities were. In a state of trance he could receive messages from what would identify as a source at times and other times it would give a name and even a bit of history from its past. The details from the experiences became so vivid and clear that the findings were undoubtedly from another energy or spirit. During one of Cayce's trances he was able to give specific details of a recipe for a medical cure. The ingredients were to be mixed and given to the patient in certain quantities. One of the ingredients was said to be located in a pharmacy in another state hundreds of miles away. The attendees of the reading contacted the pharmacy to specify the ingredient needed but the pharmacist said that it was not there. They asked Cayce again as to the location of the ingredient and the response was again the same as before, on a shelf, in the back behind several bottles. When the pharmacist looked again, it was found in a bottle way in the back all covered in dust. This was just one instance in which Cayce used an energy outside of himself to receive knowledge of something way beyond his knowing. Many of Edgar Cayce's experiences were documented by several independent and credible people leaving books and journals with an excellent source of information. There were times also when Cayce would receive details that simply could not be from any of his own recollection. When we read or listen to the documentation of these readings, we can't help but to wonder if they are real and if they are than who were the energies that were giving him the information. If these energies or spirits were from the past, than does this give us an idea as to where we go when we die? Could this other dimension be right here on earth but out of the vision and understanding of us as humans? The best way to approach these things would be to know all of the possibilities out there and then go with what feels right to you. The idea is to allow you to have a lot of options in front of you and than let you make your choice. But the fact of the matter is that more and more findings that are so close to undeniable are pointing to the evidence of energies and spirits among us, communicating through our own energy and sub-consciousness as well as through our daily activity. The point behind this is not to elaborate on psychic mediums or for you to hold trances in your living room, but to see more evidence of the energies that are available for our use. Not that we will close our eyes and take a deep breath and the next thing we know we are being spoken to by an available spirit, but if we recognize the vastness of the world and that there is so much more to all of this than what we see, we can hear more of what we are being told.

The NDE
(Near Death Experience)

An identity of spirit

*T*hrough the study of the energy within us, that energy we can detect when hooked to monitors, we can than ask more specifically what that energy is. There have been studies through the years by some pretty well educated people that have been dismissed or not given full attention due to the topic alone. Such a huge and winding wall has been put up between physiology, psychology and spirituality. For the longest time it was difficult to get psychology and neurology to find common ground let alone adding spirituality into the mix. But the thing with psychology is, it's primarily a science with intangible concepts not unlike spirituality, although it is undeniable that the way we think can be influenced by psychological findings as well as spiritual influence.

Let's take the concept of spirit. When we think of this spirit or soul that we have, it becomes a mythical perception and is difficult to envision as a shape, color or size. When I was a kid my dad worked as an electrical contractor and wired houses and small businesses. I would go along with him and watch as he toiled with the many wires and plugs throughout the job site. I remember him using a tool called an *amprobe* that would go around wires without actually touching them and would give a reading of radiated energy. The probe would detect an existence of energy although it was not able to be seen. Other tools can be used to detect electrical outlets by placing the device by, but not touching the plug and a reading will display. The point is that energy in many forms is all around us but not seen. What makes any intangible object believable is the consistency in the accounts of study. Of course if you would rather stick your finger in a light socket to determine if there was electricity going to it than help yourself, but that would be highly unrecompensed and may lead to using your near death experience in this book. Near Death Experience (NDE) is a study that can help us further understand the energy of spirit and soul.

So many of us wonder what happens to us after death but the only real way to track that would be by those who have left their human flesh and returned to tell the story. The amazing thing is the vast amount of people that have experienced these events. The objective here is to get a clearer picture of what happens to the energy from our bodies when we die. The monitors at a patient's bedside will display no reception of energy and the heart will stop beating upon death. The electrical stimulus once found through the heart has gone but where? NDEs have shone a light on this with a very acceptable option. Time after time people have been clinically dead and then have come back to life and been able to give detailed accounts of their experience. Dr. Jeffrey Long has studied these patients for many years and developed a web site and a foundation called the Near Death Experience Research Foundation that will allow for people with experiences to answer a questionnaire to further document the NDE. Dr' Long also has written a book called *Evidence of the Afterlife*, The Science of Near Death Experience that goes into further detail on the NDE and his finite studies into the patients themselves. These instances take place in many locations including operating rooms in hospitals all around the world. These documentations are clear and consistent with each other even tough they come from people thousands of miles apart and at different times in history. Dr. Long has spent a lot of time and efforts to gather as much data as possible for us to see the evidence of life after death. Over thirteen hundred accounts have been analyzed resulting in findings from genuine people that have told their stories and displayed heartfelt compassion for their experiences. One woman described leaving her body and watching herself from above and then described in detail a mans shoe she had seen from outside of the hospital. The shoe she said was blue in color with a scuff mark and was a very clear specific image. Later a nurse had been curious enough to look through all of the hospital windows and ended up finding the shoe exactly how the woman described. In another experience a patient had described leaving the body and going down the hall outside of her room and listened to the family and medical staff discussing her condition. When the patient came back to consciousness a day later, she was able to recite the conversation back to both the staff and the family although none of the words were exchanged anywhere near hearing distance from the patient. In yet another instance, a patient was passing and was standing among the family members at the bedside. It was clear to the passing patient that the family members were in mourning and recognized their pain. Not only did this person affiliate the family member's grief with emotion, he also knew that in time they would see that he was no longer in pain. In order to get a full understanding of these cases we need to break them down a little. First we know that there is an energy within the physical body that is monitored by the equipment at the patient's bedside. That energy clearly comes to a halt when the heart stops beating and the patient dies. Clinical death is described as the loss of monitored heart beat and the deletion of energy detected from the brain. It is at this point that the patients have all described some sort of out of body experience. Previously I stated the study results of the patients loosing about an ounce of weight at passing. From these accounts, at the point of death they have left their bodies and specifically recalled going to other places around them. After their NDE they are sent back to their bodies at which point the monitors reestablish an energy reading and the heart begins to beat again.

Physiologically we know that the energy has left the body at the point of dying and returns at some point. The energy or spirit that has gone out of the body retains an amazing amount of individuality. Time after time, the statements from the people going through this experience have referred to themselves as "*I* was going..." or "*I* was watching..." and it is clear that the individual was recognizing themselves still as the person they were but in a different form. Not only have they seen things through the vision of themselves but also recognize people they know around them that are still alive. This shows the ability for the spirit to retain information and remain, for a period of time that we know, themselves. They describe doing things and seeing things as we would standing here now. Over one thousand instances have been documented and they all are very similar in the recollection of their experience. I mean they don't only remember something happening but they have a *memory* of it. This would further show that in the state of the out of body experience the visions and experiences even the words heard were retained in a form of memory so that when the person returned to consciousness they were able to recollect the details. The woman that explained the details of the mans shoe outside of the hospital had been able to see the shoe as she was outside of her body and retained the exact description once back in her body. The memory was retained within the energy of the spirit. Not only was the memory of the details retained, the patient did this with the clear understanding as to who they were. ***The spirit is, in itself, still the person in the flesh***. This would suggest that when we die, our spirits retain our individuality. At this point the questions start rolling into our minds as to the physiologically retention of memory and the energy retained memory being together or separate or both.

Thousands of people have had an NDE and have reported several consistencies that have helped support their validity. High percentages of these people had specifically seen their human body below them or to the side of them, but no reports reflect a view of themselves *from* below their body. Many of them have seen a tunnel with lots of color and have felt the essence of being drawn to a light at the end but yet still feel completely relaxed and full of love. Several of them have also, at the final point before returning, been told by a voice that it was not time for them and to return. Some others have had the option to stay in their spiritual entities or go back to their human bodies. Majorities have described a feeling of love and complete ease during the experience and the presence of other beings. Some of these people recognize the other beings as family members that have passed years before and some are guided by an individual they don't recognize but are completely trustworthy in their presence. The descriptions of the other beings that have met them at the point of near death are also retaining a clear image of their earthly appearance. The retention of individuality is very important at this level because it shows the uniqueness of the spirit within and that it is representing what we have become in our human state. These accounts have opened up the opportunity to study the possibility of separate hemispheres of the personality, one as a definable spiritual entity that maintains the individual self but not the psychologically determined behaviors of the flesh. We can, through further examination of similar study, show a definite separation of mental awareness similar to the conscious and unconscious theories of Carl Jung. The question than is, how can we learn to get in touch with our subconscious and our spiritual side? It is thought that the energies all around us are constantly available but then how do we listen to them? Jung had specifically stressed the importance of being quiet and listening closely to the energy within us and all around us. This would not be much different than many forms of meditation that have been used for hundreds of years. Meditation has been used in the orient to focus deeply on the inner energies and the use of that energy to heal.

So many of us have lost a loved one and have wondered what has happened to them after they have passed. With the developing research into the spiritual being, we all can understand a possibility that fits the answer with more credibility than ever before. Step by step, from tangible and scientific results to the theories of the unknown we all can more closely articulate answers that have always been on the tips of our tongues but stop before their release. We want to know what is happening around us and to what extent we are influencing or being influenced by the energies around us. We want to know more about the life forms that drive birds to fly south in the winter and if that same energy exists within all living things. As human beings, we are naturally curious and that is the free will that God gave us to use to explore the universe around us. There is too much going on in our own bodies let alone the universe around us that can lead us to the acceptance of so much more and of a higher power working amongst us everywhere we look. The deeper we travel into these questions, the wider our eyes will come to the findings of great and wonderful things. Along the road to these findings there are many possibilities that can help us get there. The initial aspect of understanding the human body and the extra energy within it allows us a more tangible launching pad. From there we stepped to the understanding a bit more of the personality and the development of what characteristics are built through time to identify us as individuals. We looked at Carl Jung and his theory of unconscious and conscious beings that lie within us and how the unconscious is in essence our spirit. From there we took a glimpse at the near death experiences of many people that have reported on some amazing jaunts from the body and reflected the maintaining of individuality even during the out of body experience. These experiences have shown the retention of thoughts and memories with details that could only be gathered by leaving the flesh itself. Along these travels the consistencies are many and the specifics are plenty. Now that we are to this point, the question comes as to how and in what states are these contacts with our subconscious and spiritual self most likely to occur? We accept that the energy within us is of spiritual nature and that it has been linked to another place outside of our realms through its release at the point of death.

We have found that through near death experiences people are able to come in contact with other beings that were clearly in human resemblance but in spiritual form. If the energies that are released from our bodies remain in tact and maintain the knowledge and memory from human experience than the energies can project retained thought. We have seen that as the person goes through the NDE a significant amount of memory is retained and at the point of return the person was able to recite the experience clearly and in detail. At the point of the out of the body experience the person's recollection of the environment around them was a series of vivid and colorful scenes as well as feelings of comfort and love. Once we can determine that there are other spirit forms around us, we can further be open to their energy and knowledge. In the case of receiving information from other energies we would need to be very in tune with our ability to quiet our minds and reduce deflecting influence. As I stated earlier, the question of the separation of the subconscious and the conscious minds plays close to the reception and communication with energies beyond our own. Just how much of the memory we retain is in energy form verses the cellular retention of the brain tissue itself? The answers to this question may only be through the consistencies of NDE in which the individual maintains not only their own configuration but also retains the experience.

The Holy Spirit

With all of this being said, I think that I have come up with a super simple way to connect to the wonderful spirit and all of its potential. The most consistent documented directions we have are in the Holy Bible and the tool is through the Holy Spirit himself. I know through my research writing this book that there are opinions and theories all over the internet, church, books, seminars and so on but it seems that all of them are similar in the idea of the energy available. Whether it is in the cosmos, universe, the trees, all living things, the Holy Spirit, God or anything else, the understanding and hope is within the positivity of progressive and successful living. We can access these energies around us, which are all of the same source and we have the ability to create a relationship with them through our faith and leadership of God. The energies are of many types, strengths and with degrees of spiritual intensity and so it is necessary to attract only the ones we want. It is possible to be careless in the attraction of energies and the result could be of a not so positive experience. The direction I'm passing on in this book is the one that makes the most sense to me. Not just from the people that it is coming from but also from my personal experience. I cannot help but to believe with all of my heart that the connection to God and the willingness to dedicate oneself to the work of the Holy Spirit can and will allow a full balance in life. There are other things we can do to assist in the healthy balance of it all but the core is our faith. The New Testament uses the Greek word *charisma* to speak of the gifts of God through the Holy Spirit to Christians everywhere. The word charisma means to describe someone who has a quality to attract people through his or her personality. We would think of this as being an intangible thing as being part of someone's personality but the bible uses this as "a gift of holy grace." This reference is in just about only one spot and that is in the writing of the apostle Paul. It means "manifestation of grace", and is translated, "gifts." These gifts are the answers to the dedication through prayer and solid spiritual and healthy living we build in our lives. The gifts talked about in the Bible are actual results, answers to prayers and talents we can use. If we know someone with a talent of any kind we say they have a "gift" for it. This is the actual talent that is given to that person from the Holy Spirit. The amount of actual energy that is funneled into the activity that the person is doing very well is a result of the direction and influence of the energy they are tapped into. With that being said, the next question would be, what if a person does not at all believe in God but has talents, what energy are they tapping into as non Christians? I'm not sure the best way to know that unless we were directly chatting with God himself but truly I don't know of any gold medal winning devil worshipers. This is up to the judgment of the level of commitment one has and that is most certainly not for us to manage. But I can say that thousands of great and talented people in history and today give their recognition and thanks to God for the things they have achieved. I know from my experience that there seem to be several types of believers, fair weather Christians (those only needing God in bad times), quiet but dedicated Christians (those that live well, solid in faith but don't speak much of it), active Christians (live solid and balanced lives and participate in passing on the word of God through many types of service) and heavy Christians (those that are very animate as to their religion and are willing to shout praise at any time). The point is though to find a way to balance our lives in a comfortable way that will allow for a relationship with God and will provide your access to the Holy Spirit and the energy around us with the most comfort, calmness and consistency. We will all find that as we get stronger in our work and surly many already have a great way. It is up to us to find our own but the base structure is all the same.

For thousands of years there has been traceability to the Holy Spirit not only in the bible, but in books and scrolls and other documentation all around the world. The spirit in this case is not just a religious image but a powerful being, with knowledge, wisdom and guidance. What we want to do in this section is to explore what we know of the Holy Spirit in documentation from the bible and other places including testimony from some of the greatest minds of our time and then see how all of this can roll into our daily lives. I think for most people, including myself, when I would think of the Holy Spirit, I would think of this intangible idea, or concept, a representative of God that is in all living things. But I would not think of a link between my direct thinking and the power I have in my daily life to influence it in a positive way. To feed from the energy of the Holy Spirit in a manner that would further enforce my relationship with God and allow me a much deeper connection to the energies all around me. By going back to the beginning and understanding what the Holy Spirit is, we can follow things to the present day and see exactly how it all comes together. If we can think of the spirit of God from the beginning of creation, being all around the earth through the conception of all living things and then carry that same energy into the lives of early man and the life of Jesus Christ, we can see how the spirit is not just a religious concept but an active energy that is at work for us to tap into. If we can make energy as visual as possible, we can imagine that a mass of electrons, protons and neutrons will show itself in a state of light, a very bright light. We know that mass energy can be monitored and even seen at high levels. In relation to the bible, several scriptures state that the image of Jesus, Moses, Elijah and even God himself was displayed in a bright light. In Mark 9:3, Jesus appearance changed from the human state that he was in, into a bright light and his cloths shown like the sun. The energy that was within Christ was increased to such a magnitude that he shown as a mass of energy himself. With such an increase in energy even being close to him at that point would radiate to another person. After many years and studies of the Shroud of Turin, the ancient burial cloth of Christ, it is figured to have been burned like a film negative by a very bright light. The end result of this illumination was the figure on the cloth itself. The examining of the cloth found that no other manner of impression makes sense and that this must have been done during the resurrection. These findings further support the concept of energy being released in a magnificent form and depicting a spirit that maintained his individuality. God showed himself to Moses in the same visual of extreme bright light and was so magnificent that Moses body radiated light and was forced to wear a veil over his face for a time after because of the radiating energy. Even the Shroud of Turin, the claimed burial cloth of Jesus Christ is a prime example of a tangible result of the energy radiated from his body at the point of resurrection. There is more to cover with this as this section carries on but the point in the beginning is to show how all of this comes together for us now. The power of the Holy Spirit is accessible through our faith and our willingness to receive the ability to *think* in the manner in which allows for this energy to come to us. All through the bible as well we can read on the way we are supposed to think using the Holy Spirit. This is an actual method of connecting to this energy by using our minds. We are told how to use this power by focusing on the right things which opens our minds to all of the extra potential that the Holy Spirit offers. The bible actually gives details and steps to use to access this energy. All we have to do is understand it and then receive it. The energy that is in our human bodies, the physiological, measurable energy, is also linked to the energy of the Holy Spirit and when in line and connected to it, the possibilities are unbelievable. Many of the disciples and even non disciples were given the power to perform miracles by using this power. Jesus performed many healings time and time again by the amazing energy within him. Another example was when Christ walked through a crowd of people in Matthew 9:18-26, a woman wanted to be healed so she reached out to touch his cloths, when she did Jesus stopped and asked who touched him because he felt the energy leave him. Jesus had performed many miracles and the witnesses had made many clear depictions of the events and documented them. If we think of the concept of energy and the manipulation of matter, some of these events may be more broken down into details rather than just mysterious acts. If enough energy could be focused on a specific area of the body, an increase in the cell reproduction can take place. Through the reproduction of healthy cells, the damaged cells can be replaced by healthy ones in essence healing the sickness. In other cases Christ was witnessed by several people healing the sick and doing things that seem to be impossible. The energy within Christ was much more intense and the ability to use a full mind in the focus of that energy made the miracles Jesus performed much easier to complete. The consistent detail to all of the miracles was the availability of energy to perform the task. Christ also said that he granted the ability to perform healings to other people by providing them with the power of the Holy Spirit. It is this energy that is circulating through everything around us today and can be accessed by the simple act of faith.

There are many more examples of this energy and the amazing strength it has all through the bible and other scriptures throughout time. First though In Genesis 1, the bible begins by stating "At that time, the ocean covered the earth and the spirit of God hovered over the waters." From the beginning of time that we know it, the spirit of God formed energy around the earth. As time had progressed, the earth then became covered with plants, trees, animals and all living things including man, but the one thing that remained the same was the spirit of God. When we think of this spirit, it is difficult to envision what that might be, although if we look close to all living things, we can see the evidence clearly. All through the Bible, Jesus never referred to the Holy Spirit as "it" but "He" or the "Gift of The Holy Spirit". In John 16: 13 it states "When the Spirit of truth comes, he will guide you into all the truth; for he will not speak on his own authority, but whatever he hears he will speak and he will declare to you the things that are to come." Could this be the same kind of energy that Edgar Cayce was tapping into when he was able to receive messages of future events?

All of the trees we see growing around us and the grass on the ground, continues to grow in an upward direction even though gravity is pushing it down. If you think of an energy that is around the earth like the ionosphere, we could imagine that the trees are actually growing outward from the earth's surface towards the energy that is drawing it. This would explain the pattern of growth we see of most plants and trees. This energy is so strong that it also maintains the energy closer to the surface of the earth. All living things on this planet were created by God. After closely looking at the amazing human body alone, it is difficult for me to think of any possibility other wise. Considering this, than we could imagine the energy of all living things would be, in turn, attracted to the energy that created it in the first place, one energy drawn to another. This is the same for all of the energies of the universe, even us. Our energies are drawn towards not only each other, but when we are in tune with the Holy Spirit; we are drawn to him as well, linking all living things together by the power of energy.

Our sub-conscious energy is by nature spiritual therefore our energies by nature would be drawn to the spirit. The more that we are in line with the spirit, the closer we will be to the energy that surrounds us.

When Jesus was preparing to leave this earth from his human form as a man among us, he knew that his disciples were sad that he was leaving and wanted to comfort them. Jesus told them that he had to leave in order for the helper to come and guide them the rest of the way. He said "But now I am going to Him who sent me; and none of you asks me 'Where are you going?' But because I have said these things to you, sorrow has filled your heart. But I tell you the truth, it is to your advantage that I go away; for if I do not go away, the Helper shall not come to you; but if I go, I will send Him to you" (John 16: 5-7)

Jesus told us this so that he could help us understand on a simple basis that there was going to be an entity that would be available for us as a guide and resource here on earth. It was also written in Galatians 5: 16, "So I say, live by the Holy Spirits power. Then you will not do what your sinful nature wants you to do." The more we look into the bibles passages; we can find the text that provides direction for actually using this energy. What is trying to be passed to us in this writing is that we, as humans will be drawn to sinful ways because of our nature. The power of the Holy Spirit is the tapping into of the energy that God has left for us. We can directly do this by being in tune with our lives and with God. The draw for us to do the wrong thing is negative and can influence a person just as much and maybe even more than the positive. As the energy of possitivity exists, so does that of negativity. We surly can and must respect that if the power of goodness exists then also does that of evil. When we are attracted to the wrong things or tempted to do things that are by nature sinful, it is due to the influence of that negative energy around us. What we are to do, is by using the tools of the bible, build the positive strength of the spirit within us in order to deflect the influence of negativity around us. We can do this through the practice of *thought*. This is perhaps the biggest key to the entire equation. As we have looked at meditation and deep thought in the past sections of this book, we can see how the depth of thought allows for a stronger connection to the energy around and within us. The bible refers to the power of thought in Romans 8:6, "The way a sinful person thinks leads to death. But the mind controlled by the spirit brings life and peace." We know that when we actively think, we generate tangible energy from our brains creating though forms, if those thought forms are of negative structure than this is, what is referred to in this scripture as the way a sinful person thinks. But if a person creates positive thought forms than the result will be a mind controlled by the spirit bringing life and peace. The positive energy of thoughts released from our minds is attracted to and receives the positive energy of the Holy Spirit.

Here is what this opportunity offers to you and to all of us.

Steps by Step

How anyone can do this

Now that we are here at this point, the question remains as to how can anyone do this and where do we start. I'm sure this book was picked up and read by people that had an interest in understanding more of what is out there. What we can do to enlighten our lives and spirit energies to enjoy this life to its fullest. We must have a willingness and a drive to seek more and to remove from our lives the burdens and shadows that have kept us from becoming the mothers, fathers, brothers, sisters children and friends that we have always wanted to be. I began this quest with the desire to become a man that my children would look up to one day and be proud of whom he became. I wanted more than anything to find a way of life that would bring me joy and strength, comfort and wisdom in a balanced and fortified manner. My end result became a balance between mind, body and spirit and a triad of equal and unrestrained focus. The only way to achieve success at this or in any other program of life enhancement is through true and dedicated performance and drive. We must be willing to expose to ourselves the shadows that cause the bogging of our success in life. The luggage that has been strewn over our shoulders for many years been disqualifying us from the true adventures in life. With that willingness, hope and faith we can use some very simple steps to achieve what we have wanted for so long.......the best life possible.

I have broken down the steps into the following and have only put down the things that have worked for me in my life and those around me. None of this is theory alone but tools that many people have used and have found them to be an excellent avenue to enlightenment.

Recognition It is imperative that we recognize several things when we start this venture. The first is that we cannot live this life to its fullest on our own. We must realize that in order to reach the goals that we set forth, we need to be willing to accept help from all around us. The energy that we have been given access too is everywhere around us and to it we need to look for help and guidance. We as human beings have not and will not be successful without the influence of God. We have been given a pipeline of knowledge and wisdom directly from the energy mass that we came from and were created by; therefore it is only common sense that we turn to it for assistance and strength through our venture in life enhancement. If anyone looking to this plan is not willing to do this first recognition than I am afraid that this travel may not be the best one to apply. I have found that I have achieved so much more since I have used God in my life than ever before and the structure of this plan strongly includes faith and prayer. The first steps include the removal of access baggage and the willingness to turn our lives over to the care of God. This is the most powerful launch into the accessibility of energy and the backbone to the efforts I am proposing. So at this point we are open to the ideas of a new life and willing to give up our wrong doings and will examine our shadows within. So if you are still with me and have not given up here, then away we go.

At this point, right now as you read this book, I would like you to stop after this paragraph and close your eyes and take a deep breath. Focus only on the inside of your chest. Think clearly of the baggage on your shoulders, the weights slung over your neck, the chains binding your ankles and prepare to shed each and everyone of them with request to God and the Holy Spirit. At this point say "My God, through the Holy Spirit, please release these burdens from me and give me strength." Take another deep breath and feel the weights leave your body and now, at this time, your new life will begin. You can make this request as many times as you want until you begin to feel yourself come to truly understand what you are saying. Through out the Bible we are told we can receive wisdom and knowledge by requesting it from God. With a true heart we can pray for this to help guide us through this work. Billy Graham believes that this wisdom and knowledge can also bind the skills and information that we already have within and apply these things in the work that we do in the future. By retrieving what we already know and combining it with what we are given through energy we can have much more success in the ventures we are taking. So the request for knowledge and wisdom can be part of your prayers as well. Not just during times of self study but in every day endeavors. At this point we have given our will over to God and asked him for help. We are beginning our venture into the rest of our lives. It is important to use this saying, or even create your own to transmit a consistent request for guidance each day. God waits patiently for us to say hello each day, so this may be your best way to begin each dawn. Previously in this book I had noted that you can use a music pendulum to imagine your connection to the energy. In life we are a lot of the time way to the left or right of center and very seldom do we align with where we want to be. When we do hit the middle we are at the most positive position for receiving the energy that we are seeking. When we begin our days with the request for guidance we are already beginning with our first daily connection to the center point we seek. The more often we are able to align with this energy, the more influenced by it we will be. We need to build our relationship with the energy through a strong base of positive thinking and pure ways of living. As this gets more firm the energy we align with will create a passage that will flow freely through our conscious and un-conscious states. This admittance of our negative side and our wrong doings is a chance to change our lifestyles by allowing the influence of the energy to assist us. It is absolutely necessary to do this with a whole heart and truly expect to devote your attention and effort to this opportunity. The more directly you make these efforts the more specific the results will be. Also the amount of time that it takes for you to see and feel these changes also will shorten with the dedication you put forth.

This first real step into the changing of your life is the most important and can be built stronger every day that you repeat this. Within a short period of time you will feel a calmness come over you and you will feel the actual energy within you begin to change. The activity within the energy will increase and start to make a shift towards a new direction. You will begin to feel yourself become more curious as to the surroundings around you. This is the recognition of the Holy Spirit that your internal energy is making a connection too. In the same way that the tones of music, when structured correctly, can ignite a frenzy of excitement within the energy, the connection with the Holy Spirit is also a calmness of home. In the cases of Near Death Experiences, the patients had explained an amazing feeling of calmness and love when they approached the other side. This is the same energy that is connected to us when we are in tune with God; the exact place that receives us is also where we came from so the soul's recognition of this energy will be the same as we become in touch with it in a human form. This is why the request to God is so important, because it is by his blessing that we are received into the heaven that is prepared for us which is also at the end of the portal that is described by those that have had these NDEs. The point is that when people have experienced this connection to another place after death and are able to all relate their feeling to those of understanding, love and completeness, than we are also able to connect to that same energy when we are still alive just not to the extent as being passed to the other side. We are able to connect to the energy here on earth but not completely engulf ourselves until it is our time to travel to that place in the passing of death. The key here again is to fully give yourself over to be available for the gifts of the Holy Spirit.

At this point we have begun shifting from the right or left and begun the pendulum swing towards the center. The next step is to identify the shadows of our internal being, I call this **Shadow Dissection.**

Our ego and the closets that hide what is necessary to expose and evaluate our shadows can be for a lot of people, including myself very difficult. We are going into a deeper understanding of who we are as individuals and will develop a firm view of the person inside. Most of the time we don't properly address our feelings or recognize what it is that our subconscious is trying to tell us through our feelings and emotions. A further understanding of our shadows opens the door to the opportunity to place in order the files that have been left alone or ignored for many years or not even opened. Through this process I was slow to open the closets that held the most influential parts of my life. The death of my son and the accident that took the life of my best friend had contributed massively to the growth of my shadow and the behavior that affected my capabilities as a father, son friend and husband. I spent a week end at a center for life enhancement that gave me the perfect opportunity to understand these feelings and the destruction that would continue if I didn't do something about them. I was able to recognize exactly what it was that I was feeling and then ask myself what impacts have those instances had on me and my productivity. I also carried it deeper into asking myself why I allowed these feelings to continue to be active in my life. At the end of the weekend I was not cured of the pain that the losses incurred but was aware of what they were. I was able to accept their passing and use many tools to enjoy my memories and even go and visit them in my meditations. Once this was put into a clearer understanding I was able to then look at how these things have effected the other ways of thinking that I had structured over the years due to the negative draw of energy that captivated my potential.

This took several years to modify and understand the complete thought structure that I had built and then began to modify it in stages of importance. A simpler way to start this would be to begin with a list. Actually take a pen and paper and sit down quietly by yourself and write down everything that you feel has influenced you the most, positive and negative. Make a separate list for both. Remember that when you do this, no one else need be involved. This is only for yourself to begin a base point for the rest of the work ahead. Remember the more truthful you are with yourself the more successful you will be as this venture continues. Your list is for you to have hidden away for now and not to be shared with anyone else. As a matter of fact it would be better if you told no one of the work you are doing. This can be tough in the beginning and there are always negative input from the outside that can hinder the progress you are making. The others can find out in time. As you make your list, again being as truthful as possible, you may be surprised with the size of the list itself. What is happening within you is an increase in mind and thought activity due to the heightened energy. As you are making these efforts to improve your life, you are accessing already the energies of the universe which will increase the internal energy within you which then in turn increases the physiological capabilities of memory and self awareness. The energy that is released during the creation of thought forms can be increased at this point which will speed up the brains capabilities and increase the lobe depth and thought strength. This is also when things start to get fun. When you become firmer into the connection with the energy the ideas and visions will come quicker and more vivid. Also the creativity during this process will increase and will assist you with the details and the source of the ideas, feelings and thoughts that will come flooding into your mind and funnel onto the paper before you.

Although this step is covered over just a matter of a few pages, it can take quite a while to actually complete or even begin to filter through these issues. Sometimes these things can take several years and along the way you will find yourself becoming emotional on both sides of the tracks and a wide variety findings are possible but this cleaning out of closets is valuable to the success of this work. As I rummaged through all of the corners of my closet I found myself uncovering things that were put away long ago. One of the great things during this process is that the energy within is working with you to assemble pieces of issues that may never have been identified. When we find feelings or issues we don't understand, the subconscious energy will work with the physiological mind to put all of the pieces together and allow you to put labels on the folders as you create them. A wonderful tool along this work is the "Serenity Prayer, God grant me the serenity to accept the things that I cannot change, the courage to change the things that I can and the wisdom to know the difference." While evaluating these issues that have and will affect your life the most, this prayer will allow you to understand what to spend the most time on and how to organize them. For example, my son's passing was a major impact on my life and as I identified it I had to ask myself what the issue was doing to me. I found that I was hanging onto his life and not allowing myself to accept that he was gone. Once I realized that I had to ask myself why I was not letting go of his death and the answer was linked to the death of my friend Eric. I had named my son after my best friend and had placed a lot on my son's life because I wanted to still hang onto my friends name and memory through my son. Loosing my son had extended my lose of my friend and also made it worse by adding the pain of my sons death as well. Once I was able to realize what I was doing with this in a subconscious manner, I was able to use the Serenity Prayer to organize my feelings for Eric and Matthew. I could clearly not change the passing of either one of them but I could change the way that I held onto their memory. I found a place for Eric and Matthew and was able to let go of the guilt and pain that was intertwined with the good parts of their lives. In this case for example, I can come to a full recognition with these feelings and be able to keep their memory in my life in a positive way rather than having it all effect me negatively through the clouded vision that I chose to see them before. This is one instance in which the shadow within me was dissected and a piece was re-formed and placed into a positive form. The "Why" rule can also help through this process. This is when we identify a feeling that affects us strongly and we ask ourselves *why* five times to go back deeper into the shadow to find the source of the feeling and where it originated from.

It is very important to recognize all of our feelings every day because God gave us the ability to feel pain and joy and everything in between. If we are not feeling sad or recognize what we feel sad about, we are denying the gift that God gave us of allowing emotions to influence us. Without love we won't feel sadness and won't recognize joy or anger. The great thing is that we are naturally spiritual and the closer we get to the Holy Spirit the more in tune we will get of the feelings we feel and can see more of what makes us tick. I have had friends that have been developing their self image and individualization for five plus years and just recently have come to a solid ground with their inner being. Though this is not an over night job, once we begin we will find drastic changes rather quickly. The work is long and difficult but the positive enforcement delivered from the outer energies will be recognized in the early stages of your efforts. At this stage there is no problem seeking professional assistance in any aspect of this plan. We must learn to take advantage of our resources and not be afraid to use assistance to achieve our goals.

At this point, if the prayers for assistance from God and the Holy Spirit have been isolated and shadow dissection has been started, than you certainly have felt and experienced a change within you already. The level of inner self recognition can be in the early stages and can continue for years while moving on through more steps. So at this juncture we can move on while still working on other things. As we are gathering knowledge through this work we can pull it from many different places. There are many books out there that can provide some wonderful tools and each one you add to your arsenal is valuable. Earlier I spoke of Billy Graham, his book *The Holy Spirit*, is a great way to come to a more constructive understanding of what that energy is and how to use it. This book goes into an easy and yet clear, firm depiction of the Holy Spirit, history of him, and the connection to other aspects of the Bible. Of course the Bible itself is a necessary part of any of this work but it is difficult to read it like a book from the front to the back but if you have the time you certainly can do that. Another way you can experience the Bible is to use the internet or computerized version of the Bible. By being able to search fro specific words or topics, you can go directly to the spot that you want to read up on. The most commonly read books of the Bible are Genesis and Revelation. The first and the last books because it is the easiest and most drawn to books of the Bible but so much more can be found as you know where to look.

As each person goes along this path there will be things that come faster to some than to others but the end result is the same. With this work an amazing finding will come, a realization that there is so much more going on around us than we all ever thought and that it came from a source so great and beyond that we cannot and will not ever comprehend it all. But the fact is this, each and every one of us have the potential to align with the same energy that has been here for centuries. We must find a completeness within ourselves and see that our venture is to assist mankind in its movement forward towards harmony and success. This is most certainly possible with the access and use of the Holy Spirit's energy. The Bible even tells us that the information from the Spirit is one of knowledge, wisdom and future events. Many people throughout time have used this great power and made phenomenal changes in others lives and that is what we are here to do.

As we come down to a calmness within ourselves we need to maintain a consistent connection with the universe and the Spirit. Our daily activities can crown our minds with un-needed distraction so we will need to find ways to filter out what is useful and not so useful, damaging and strengthening. Each day we encounter a rollercoaster of emotion and influence. The energy around us is trying to communicate to us at the same time that the chaos of the day pulls our attention elsewhere. It is through this that we must find balance and remain true to our convictions. The closer we get to the Spirit, the easier these things will become. The busy day will become one of function and enlightenment and the struggle to adapt will fall to the wayside. Meditation is a wonderful tool to use while we are starting, going through and certainly closing our days. I have covered a bit of meditation in the past sections but this is a tool for me as well as for you and there are a lot of methods available. I am a vessel for God to use here and so I use what I find along the way. I am not, by far, an expert in anything except my determination. There are plenty of great people available for in depth information on meditation and its history but I can give you an idea as to simple methods used by every day people along their paths. Here is a meditation technique and some words that you may enjoy as you enter into a calm relaxing mode.

Our minds need to become at a center of relaxation and equality. A proper space is important for meditation although you can do it just about anywhere. The ideal way to do this is by preparing a special location just for this. A quiet and relaxing spot in your house is perfect, one that you can make your very own and feel at complete peace. Your mind will associate the location with peace and immediately put you there as you begin. Don't meditate in bed because it is too easy to fall asleep. This can be done anywhere if you can associate the location with peace and relaxation. It is not the location as much as it is the state of mind that you enter by being in that place. Correct posture and breathing is essential in this practice but making yourself uncomfortable will not help. Sitting straight and on a comfortable surface is ideal but if you find a position that more suits you I think that will be fine as well. Focus on your breathing and bring yourself to a place of oneness with your inside being. Your breath is the sound of your inner self relaxing and becoming open to energy. Once in a place of relaxation, you can add Affirmations, or statements that will enforce positive thought. Some good ones I use are "I release ego, I release judgment, and I release my fear of disappearing." "I am Gods servant and I have faith in Love." You can use anything that you wish to deeper enforce your structure as to who you are and want to be. This is what you become. You become exactly what you think the most of in this state. The subconscious will pick this up and further adapt it in your daily living. Mantras are also an excellent method of meditation adaptation. The most popular mantra is OM. From Hindu it is pronounced "A-OO-M". The Hindus believe that the sound vibrations from this connect to the sound of creation of the universe. As I had mentioned earlier, sound and music has a way of delivering deeper connection to energy by connecting to the vibrations of the source of all. Again there are many ways to meditate and a lot of information available for you. The point again with this is for us to find a way to stop and hush the outside world and listen to the energy and the Spirit around us. This is the deliverance of so much wisdom and knowledge that we will be astounded as to its abilities. Once we become at peace with ourselves and the shadows are dissipating, we will find such an enlightenment in each day that we become new and awake in the energy and Spirit we are given.

Coming Home, Awake, Aware,
Excited and Loved

Along the pages of this book, I wanted you, the reader, to be able to take a step away from the ordinary and most commonly chaotic world that we live in and see that there is truly something more out there for us. As we look at the human body and all of the miracles that happen inside of us each millisecond of every day, we can't help but to believe in the unbelievable mind of a great creator we call God. So many pieces of our structure and the wiring along the brain, across the brain stem and out to the very tips of our fingers bring us deeper into a realization that this body we are using is a miracle and gift alone. If the creation of such an amazing, rugged but delicate vessel has been designed and given to us for travel along this life than such an amazing creator must have plans for us after we leave this planet. We have seen through near death experiences that our spirits are individuals themselves and retain memory as well as unique character after it leaves the shell of the body, so we cannot help but believe that another place is waiting for us and our loved ones as they carry on away from us. With the universe around this planet, it is crazy to think that there is no other life anywhere out there in the vastness of billions of stars and planets and therefore it would be thought that it sure would be a waste to be turned to dust after we pass away and nothing more exists after all of the wonderful things we see around us. We have to stop and realize that the things happening within us are unanswerable miracles, like the beating of our hearts and the energy that is supplied mysteriously to assist it hundreds of times each day and the electrical pulse that streams down the fibers inside giving movement and stimulation to the slightest touch on a finger tip.

There is simply way too much going on with our bodies to deny the existence of its creator and the gifts that come along with it. Like the human body, the psychology of individualism can only answer so much, leaving the remainder of questions to theory but a theory of great possibility and hope. Our individualism, personality and character cannot come from the development over time alone, or just by the influence from the outside world but from a spirit energy inside of us coming from a place beyond our comprehension. As we are maintained by an energy that we cannot deny and that we know that it must have a spiritual source than we again have to accept the idea of an afterlife. There are books upon books of theory and far out thinking, of genuine attempts to answer the questions lingering for all time and those that go above and beyond anything that we request, but only one has stood the test of time as one of consistency and devotion and that is the Bible. Along all of these travels, thousands of people have referred to this book for answers and understanding, for clues and guidance and certainly for love and faith in the hope for something more great than our birth, life and passing to dust. We have been given a light on our path, an access to the energy of our creator which is our link to the entire universe of answers and power. Like we cannot deny the existence of unexplained energy within us we also cannot pass on the documentation of our energy. The spirit within us is that of the Holy Spirit and is drawn to it each and every day. We would be foolish not to want to adapt our lives to funnel this energy which is full of wisdom and knowledge into our very souls. All of this was and is connected to the vibrations and attraction of the world and beyond. The heavens that we see through telescopes and technology are also the source of millions of individual energies freely passing to and from our world. We can hear them when we listen, when we are in tune with the Spirit we are also in tune with positive, genuine and helpful spirits beyond us. The concept of all of this is to once again accept that this all cannot be as simple as the mutation of a pond creature and that we are, in physical form, a miracle. Once we admit to that we can accept the concept of divine creation. There is just no way that the scientifically unanswered questions of the existence of internal energy and its functions can be dismissed as whoopla any longer. Once we can admit to our undeniable creation we can absorb the theory of spiritual release at death and the existence of another place after life. All of this can be an acceptable and willing proposition with the removal of blinders and skepticism. We as wonderful and amazing human beings, housing our special and intriquet spiritual energies, must now give up our singleness of life and say ok to our meaning. Say ok to what we are here for and quit perpetuating along a directionless road filled with loss and disappointment. This life and world has never been and never will be a bed of roses but with this acceptance and will to apply what we have been given for thousands of years, we can LIVE, truly and undeniably LIVE. We can provide, we can give and receive, we can invent, we can paint, we can produce and teach, we can run and dance, we can sit and talk and thanks to God and the Spirit, we can LOVE and be LOVED. We have a responsibility to ourselves and to mankind, to move us all forward as closely as possible. Assist one another to enjoy life and to recognize the gifts that the Holy Spirit is offering. The wonders and amazing chapters of knowledge and wisdom waiting to zoom into our minds and give us light along a pathway of individual darkness. We are here my friends, each day, each minute and every second is our time. Once again I ask you to join me. Let go of the weights of life and ego, let go of pain and suffering and let free the guilt and forgive once and for all. Accept God, pray and ask for his guidance through the energy of the Holy Spirit and feel the ability to release and enjoy your children and your parents, your brothers and sisters, your grandparents, cousins and friends. Be the wife you have always wanted to be and the husband so many wait for you to become. Be the person you have always hoped to develop into before it is too late. Your time is now! Awaken! Smile! Breathe! YOU ARE LOVED! By the grace of God.........We are loved!